FLY FISHING
TECHNIQUES
& TACTICS

FLY FISHING TECHNIQUES & TACTICS

LEFTY KREH

THE LYONS PRESS
Guilford, Connecticut
An imprint of The Globe Pequot Press

Copyright © 2002 by the Lyons Press
Photography by:
Val Atkinson/Frontiers (pages 132, 140/141)
Dan Blanton (pages 40/41)
Lefty Kreh (pages 8, 14, 20/21, 26, 60/ 61, 92, 148)
Bob Lewis (frontispiece)
Jim Teeny (pages 11, 49, 52, 124)

Illustrations by Rod Walinchus

ALL RIGHTS RESERVED. No part of this book may be reproduced or transmitted in any form by any means, electronic or mechanical, including photocopying and recording, or by any information storage and retrieval system, except as may be expressly permitted by the 1976 Copyright Act or in writing from the publisher. Requests for permission should be addressed to The Globe Pequot Press, P.O. Box 480, Guilford, Connecticut 06437.

The Lyons Press is an imprint of The Globe Pequot Press.

Printed in the United States of America.

2 4 6 8 10 9 7 5 3

The Library of Congress Cataloging-in-Publication Data is available on file.

ISBN 1-58574-505-7

CONTENTS

INTRODUCTION

To successfully catch fish — especially larger fish — on fly tackle means properly attending to a number of things between the time you decide to make a trip until the final release of your fish. Many surveys reveal that 10 percent of fly fishermen catch 90 percent of the fish, and I endorse that finding. For I am one of those anglers who believes that there is very little luck involved in successful fly fishing. You make the most of your own luck — good or bad.

Properly preparing your tackle, being at the right place at the best time, knowing how to approach and position yourself in relation to the fish (whether you are fishing from shore, wading or approaching from a boat or canoe), casting effectively, making the right fly presentation and retrieve, then striking, fighting, landing and releasing the fish: these are not matters of luck, but learned skills: the techniques and tactics of fly fishing.

In this book, I'll be discussing how I believe you can improve your performance in all of these areas, excepting casting technique — the foundation of all fly fishing — to which several books have already been devoted. For a complete discussion of casting, see *Longer Fly Casting,*

◄ *Irv Swope executing a careful cast and presentation to a wily brown trout on Greenspring, a limestone stream in south central Pennsylvania.*

Saltwater Fly-Casting Techniques, or *Solving Fly-Casting Problems.*

Speaking of other books, as you read this one, you will see it is more or less a general survey of a number of important techniques for increasing your chances of success in fly fishing in a number of tactical situations, to many types of fish.

You might call it "Techniques and Tactics 101," because even though some of the ideas I'll be sharing with you are fairly sophisticated concepts that are used generally only by very experienced fly fishermen, they are set forth to provide you — regardless of your level of ability — with a broad and solid foundation in what I regard as being some of the most important techniques of fly fishing.

But these are by no means all the techniques that need to be mastered to achieve fly fishing proficiency. There are many, many more — some of them quite specialized.

When you think about it, you could say that almost all of the books that have been written about fly fishing in the last four hundred years or so — I'm talking about thousands and thousands of pages — are really about nothing else but techniques and tactics!

So I wouldn't presume to tell you that the information contained in the pages of this small book is all you're going to need to become a fly-fishing master. But I do believe that what you're going to read in these pages is sound, practical, and most of all, *effective* information that you can begin to use *right now*, on your very next fishing trip, no matter where you're going or what species of fish you'll be fishing to, in fresh or saltwater.

A selection of flies for Alaska. Experienced anglers prepare their equipment in advance of a trip, as Lefty will discuss in Chapter One. ➤

I hope, also, that you will find a lot of this information to be new — or at least that it will provide you with valuable insights into techniques you are already using. Otherwise, I'm wasting my time and your money. If you reach that conclusion, if I were you I'd return the book to the publishers and get my money back. But of course, I hope you won't want to!

Regarding the more specialized techniques and tactics that need to be mastered for fly fishing to specific species of fish — trout, bonefish, permit, tarpon, steelhead, salmon, etc., our plan for the Library is to bring you that information in separate books that will be coming to you soon.

Something else I think is worth saying. Those of you who know me, know that I'm not a traditionalist. Now I have nothing against tradition. In fly fishing we have a great one. And I get as much pleasure as any traditionalist, I suppose, from making upstream presentations to trout with a bamboo rod, light tippet, and dry fly.

But the fly fisherman's world has changed. Convenient jet air travel has opened up the entire world for fly fishing adventure to fishing hot spots and fish species unknown to us a generation ago, many of which can only be tackled successfully with newly developed techniques and tactics. And modern tackle technology — particularly in the area of rods and lines — makes possible casting feats that were previously beyond the reach of all except the professional. It continues to amaze me, for example, to see what just a moderately proficient fly caster can accomplish today on big water with a state-of-the-art graphite rod and a specialized fly line!

Also, more than ever before, anglers are discovering the special pleasures of saltwater fly fishing. As you may have noted, the subtitle of this book indicates that we will be examining fly fishing in both fresh and saltwater.

Now I am aware that many of you may have never fished in the salt, nor may you ever intend to. But even so, I think you should at least take a look at the saltwater material in the book. For while the freshwater angler may never need the experienced saltwater fly fisherman's skill in casting into heavy ocean breezes or at extremely long distances, for many other important fly-fishing techniques — such as approaches, presentations, retrieving, striking and landing fish — I have found that fly fishing in saltwater has substantially improved my technique for all other types of fishing. Saltwater wisdom has many valuable freshwater applications.

I hope this material will help you towards achieving your overall fly-fishing goal, which, if it's anything like mine, is to experience one of the world's great pleasures that I believe comes only to the fly fisherman — from first fooling fish with an artificial fly, and then catching and returning unharmed to their wild environment as many as you can (the larger the better!) in comfort and safety, and with skill and sportsmanship.

Thank you for reading what I have to say.

OVERLEAF: *Fly fishermen returning at sunset from a great day of bonefish and permit fishing, Baypoint Park, south Biscayne Bay, Florida.*

CHAPTER ONE

PREPARING TO FISH

A great fishing trip almost always begins at home. Factors such as what kind of clothing you will use, selecting the proper rod and line, even which sunglasses you will wear, as well as selecting flies and correctly building leaders, are all actions that should be taken before your trip, at home.

DO YOUR SITE PLANNING BEFORE YOU LEAVE HOME

Pre-planning a trip is always good advice. Even if you are only going to a regional trout stream 50 miles from home, try to get up-to-date information. Call a local tackle shop, outdoor writer, friend, fish or game warden or someone who knows local conditions. Determine if certain flies are hatching, if water levels are extra low, normal, high, clear or dirty, or what tidal phases are best. Too many anglers, especially those fairly familiar with their local waters, will simply grab their tackle and drive to the scene only to find they didn't bring the right kind of tackle, could not match the great hatch that was on, or were simply there at the wrong time.

If you're planning a trip overseas or at long distance from your home, where local knowledge is not readily available, you should exercise considerable caution in your choice of location, accommodations and guides, particularly when planning a trip to such popular fly-fishing destinations as the Rocky Mountains, the Florida Keys, the Bahamas and Caribbean, Alaska, Argentina, New Zealand, etc., and even more particularly, in third-world countries After all, if things go wrong, it's your comfort, safety, health and even your life that's at stake.

Unless you plan on making all long-distance travel and fly-fishing arrangements on your own (which I don't recommend unless you simply enjoy adventuring into the unknown and are willing to accept the consequences of this type of travel), I suggest you use a reputable fly-fishing travel agent. There are plenty of good ones around. I think the best is Frontiers International (address: P.O. Box 959, Wexford, Pennsylvania 15090; telephone 800-245-1950). But I do some work for them, so you may want to take that opinion with a grain of salt. But whatever outfitter you use, require that they provide you with references of past clients so you can check them out. Don't book into an unknown fly-fishing travel deal.

All the major fly-fishing magazines carry extensive classified advertising sections listing U.S. and international destinations, lodges and guide services. But again, conduct your own investigation of these advertisers by contacting three or four fishermen who have patronized the operator before you make a final commitment and send him money. Because, as John Randolph, publisher of *Fly Fisherman* tells me, unless there is clear evidence of fraud or misrepresentation, commercial magazines really have no way to check the truth of these type of ads; and consequently they are in no position either to criticize or endorse the content of such advertisements.

Another good source of fly-fishing travel information is Don Causey's newsletter, *The Angling Report* (address: 9300 S. Dadeland Blvd., Suite 605, Miami, Florida 33156; telephone 305-670-1361).

Whatever travel plans you have made, always be sure to arrange for a local guide before you reach your fly-fishing destination. Experienced guides are not necessarily inexpensive — particularly those who have developed an international reputation and enjoy a number of repeat clients. But the cost of a knowledgeable guide will normally be far below the cost of your air travel, and usually a good guide will be the single most important contributing factor to the success or failure of your trip. If you fail to do this, you may be stuck with having to retain whatever guide is available when you get there, and if he's available on such short notice, you should wonder why!

PREPARE A TRAVEL CHECK LIST

For all your trips, foreign or domestic, you should always make yourself a travel check list. My list is rather lengthy. It includes more than 50 items — everything I would need whether I were making a trip to Alaska or to the jungles of New Guinea. If you will make a number of copies of the list and put them on a clipboard, you can use one copy per trip, modifying the basic list to meet the requirements of your upcoming trip. For example, if you are going to the Bahamas for bonefish, you will obviously not need the cold-weather clothing on your check list (which you would need if you were going to Montana in late September). Go down the check list and mark off those things you think you'll need for your next trip. If you use a check list you will rarely take a trip and forget something.

CHECK YOUR TACKLE

Tackle preparation is essential. It is the fly tackle that will deliver your offering to the fish, hook it, and finally bring it close so you can land it. If a part of your tackle is improperly rigged, you'll probably score poorly.

Select and Install Reel Backing

Fly reels are first loaded with backing, which accomplishes two purposes. First, backing allows you to put enough mass underneath the fly line so that the spool is completely filled out to its maximum diameter. This allows quicker recovery when winding in line. And, since backing permits you to store the fly line on the reel in larger coils, the line is less kinky when first pulled off the reel, and so it will tend to travel better in a straight line when cast.

Therefore the selection of good backing material, and its proper installation on the reel, are important considerations. Monofilament nylon is not considered good backing, as I will explain below. The best backing material is either squidding line (my personal favorite and difficult to obtain) or Dacron (or a very similar material, Micron).

To install backing, many people simply casually wind the backing onto their reel, then attach the fly line. That's okay if you never plan to hook a strong fish that is going to pull off a good deal of your backing. But the force exerted by a strong fish as it is escaping will pull a lot of backing off the reel that must be rewound on the spool. And if this occurs several times during the battle, and if the backing was installed casually or improperly, as the angler pumps and winds in recovering the fish, the pumping and winding action will cause the taut line, being recovered under tension, to dig deeply into the bed of line remaining on the spool. Then when the fish runs again, as line is given to the escaping fish, the spool will revolve until it reaches the point where the line is buried in the bed of backing, causing a lurch or jerk on the line, which can result in a leader break and a lost fish.

You must install the backing as tightly as possible, so that the bed of backing is so firm that the line being recovered doesn't dig into it.

And this is also the reason why I recommend that you not use monofilament for backing. For no matter how tightly you have originally installed monofilament backing on the spool, it will invariably stretch under the stress of bringing in a strong fish. And when placed back onto the reel in such a stretched or elongated condition, it will almost always embed itself into the monofilament backing remaining on the spool.

In addition, so that you can recover line faster when winding, you should always have the fly reel spool as completely filled with backing and line as is possible, right up to its maximum diameter. There is a simple way to install the line and backing to achieve a maximum fill of the spool. Instead of putting the backing on first (as many anglers do), *wind the fly line on the empty spool first*, then attach the backing to the fly line, and wind on enough backing to fill the spool to the maximum. Next, remove all the backing and fly line from the spool. Now reverse the entire procedure, winding the backing onto the spool first, followed by the fly line. You'll end up with a perfectly filled spool.

Another important consideration concerning backing is deciding what pound test to use. Keep in mind that Dacron and Micron lines in lighter weights do not stand up well to abrasion. You can prove this quickly with a little test. Take a one-foot length of 12-pound test Dacron or Micron backing and insert it in a rod guide. Have someone hold the rod while you firmly grasp the two ends of the backing protruding from the guide, and saw back and forth vigorously, causing the line to rub back and forth on the rod guide. After just 10 seconds of this back-and-forth sawing motion, examine the line, comparing it to a piece of the same line that is new. You will likely be surprised at how the tested

OVERLEAF: *Larry Foster fishing the Henry's Fork, Idaho.*

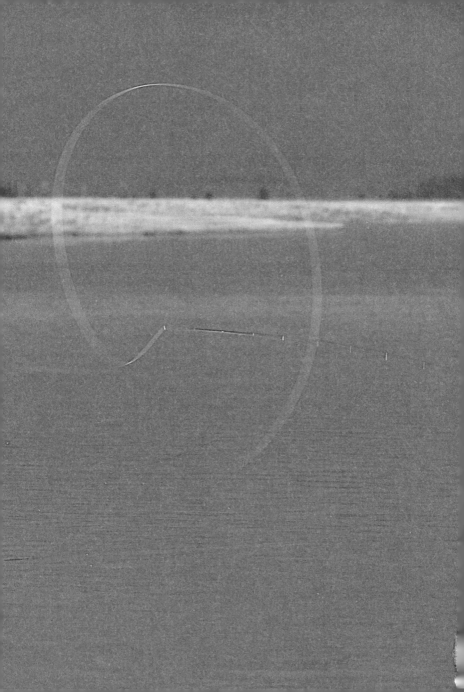

segment of line has broken down. The purpose of this experiment is to convince you that 12-pound test Dacron or Micron backing may be a little on the thin side — even for trout fishing. The lightest backing I use is 20-pound, and most of the time I prefer 30-pound.

Clean Your Fly Lines

If your fly line has been used frequently, it may be dirty. Some waters, especially large southern and mid-Atlantic rivers, will put enough dirt on a fly line in a single day to require cleaning it. A dirty floating line will not float well, and really any type of line — floating, sinking, or what have you — is difficult to shoot any distance if it's dirty.

There are two easy ways to clean a fly line that I prefer. One is to use Glide, a commercial fly line cleaner that removes the dirt quickly and gives a slick finish that permits the line to shoot better. Glide is manufactured by Umpqua Feather Merchants (address: P.O. Box 700, Glide, Oregon 97433, telephone 503-496-3512) and is available in many fly shops. To insure that the slick surface it imparts to the line will remain for a long time, *Glide should be applied several hours before using the line and allowed to dry thoroughly.*

Another method of cleaning a fly line is simply to wash it in warm water with a mild liquid dishwashing detergent. Pull the line through a sponge soaked through with the warm water/detergent mixture. Then be sure that you rinse all the detergent from the line with cold water, or else the line will not float properly.

Build Leaders Ahead of Time

Leaders are the next item to check. Many anglers will not build their leaders until they get to the fishing scene. What a waste of good fishing time! Prepare your leaders at home, where you're not distracted by the fish or the environment, and where you'll have more time to build them properly. Knots tied at home, where you're not handicapped by haste or wind, are almost always better.

Select Flies and Sharpen Hooks

Of course, the proper flies should be selected. If there is any question about whether hooks are sharp enough, touch them up with a file or hone. I believe that a very common fault of fly fishermen is that far too many fish with hooks that are not sharp enough.

CHECK YOUR AUXILIARY GEAR AND CLOTHING

Carry Polaroid Sunglasses for Sighting Fish

Most anglers are aware that using Polaroid sunglasses to eliminate glare is an essential part of seeking trout, bonefish and other species which we actually look for before making the cast. I believe that amber/brown-colored Polaroid sunglasses are to be preferred for most fishing situations, perhaps as much as 90 percent of the time.

But bear in mind that other colors may be more effective in certain situations. Polaroid sunglasses in a blue/gray tint can be very effective on bright sunlit days on a snow-white bonefish flat. Medium yellow tints can work well on smaller trout streams where the water is shaded and often difficult to see through.

Select Clothing of the Proper Color

The color of your clothing is an important consideration in fly fishing, especially when seeking trout. Trout live in clear waters and usually must be approached at close quarters before a presentation is made. I am a firm believer in having clothing that blends with the surroundings.

For example, most of the vegetation and woodlands of the Eastern U.S. is green during the warmer months when we seek trout. Yet throughout this region, anglers usually wear khaki-colored fishing vests which present a strong contrast to the local vegetation and foliage. After many years of observing this behavior, I'm convinced that in these areas if anglers wore a vest of greenish tint they would approach trout more effectively. When fishing in the East, I use RIT (or any equivalent common household dye available in most supermarkets) to dye my khaki vest to a forest green.

For fishing in the Western U.S., pack your khaki-colored vest, where it will usually blend better with the surroundings.

When fishing meadow streams, or when seeking tarpon and bonefish on saltwater flats, where the angler is generally situated against a bright sky background which the fish will be looking up and into, pale blue or green or similar light colors that blend in well with the sky are best. Even a white shirt isn't bad, since the fish frequently are looking up at white clouds.

Brightly colored hats, even those with fluorescent colors, are in vogue among many young anglers. But wearing such colors is the equivalent of flashing a mirror to tell the fish you're close by.

In fly-fishing situations where it is necessary to see the fish before casting, having the underside of your hat brim the right color is important. Certainly any hat brim will reduce glare and aid vision — the darker the better — but I prefer to use one with an underside color of solid black, which I make by simply applying black liquid shoe polish to the fabric of the underside of the brim.

Selecting properly colored clothing before you leave home is one of the important considerations to successful fly fishing.

PREPARE FOR YOUR TRIP WITH MR. MURPHY'S LAW IN MIND

Prepare your tackle and gear before you leave home and you'll substantially increase your chances for having a good fishing trip. For in fly fishing, as most of you probably already know, God knows you need the best edge you can get. Murphy's Law applies in spades to fly fishing. Sooner or later, on one of your fly-fishing trips, anything that can go wrong, will go wrong. (I've renewed my acquaintanceship with Mr. Murphy more times than I care to remember!) The commuting time from camp to your daily fishing site will always be longer than you had planned on. The wind is going to blow harder than you expected, and over your wrong shoulder. The arthritis in your back, which had given you no trouble during your couch potato months at home, will go into deep trauma at just about the time you need to be making strong double hauls to a double figure fish. It's always going to be colder, or hotter, than you expected. It will probably rain. If it doesn't rain, it will *pour*. And once you've left camp and gotten several hours up the river, you're going to discover at lunch time that someone (probably you) forgot to pack the sandwiches.

BASIC RULES FOR PREPARING TO FISH

1. Do your site planning before you leave home.
2. Prepare a travel check list.
3. Select and properly install good reel backing.
4. Clean your fly lines.
5. Build leaders ahead of time.
6. Select flies and sharpen hooks.
7. Carry Polaroid sunglasses for sighting fish.
8. Select the proper color for your clothing.

OVERLEAF: *Bob Clouser on the Susquehanna River, Pennsylvania.*

CHAPTER TWO

APPROACHING THE FISH

Once on the water and with tackle assembled, your next problem is how to approach the fish and get yourself into a good position to present your fly to it. *A cardinal rule in approaching any fish is that you should make your approach so that the fish is never aware that you are there.* Any indication that you give of your presence will put the fish on guard and make it more difficult to achieve a take.

APPROACH SLOWLY

Think *slow.* If you have ever watched a great blue heron or an egret as it stalks its dinner, you had a great opportunity to learn a valuable lesson on how to approach the fish you hope to catch. These big birds will stand motionless for long periods, and when they move, they move *very slowly.* They never make a quick movement until they are ready to grab their prey.

One of the ways that fish become aware of anglers is through their sensory organs that "feel" our presence. The ears of the fish, located in the head, as well as the lateral line along the side of their body, can detect movements in the water. These two organs allow a fish to locate a swimming baitfish, creeping crayfish or crab sneaking along the bottom in roiled water, even at night. It is not necessary for a fish to actually see its prey (or us) to be aware of our presence in its environment.

Therefore, one of the most important techniques to keep in mind when approaching any fish in calm water (whether it is a bonefish on a saltwater flat or a brown trout in a still pool) is that we must wade, like the egret, *very slowly*. By way of analogy, assume that a calm body of water is much like a balloon filled with water. If you push your finger against one side of the balloon, it forces the balloon to expand away from the finger on the other side. If you wade in calm water too quickly, the shock waves created by your wading will move through the water column, just as the effect of your finger pushing against the side of the balloon. Wade quickly and the fish will sense immediately that someone is approaching. So when wading in any calm water it's always good technique to wade slowly. If you detect ripples on the surface that are extending out more than two feet in front of your legs, then you are definitely moving too quickly.

Don't Make Waves

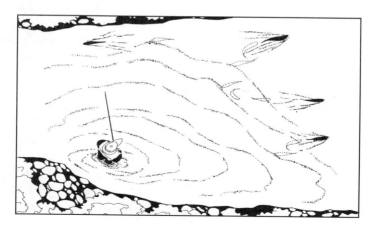

Nowhere in fishing is this violated more than when fishing for trout. Anglers will enter a rather long pool and wade rather rapidly and carelessly to within near-casting distance of a trout. Only then do they begin to slowly and quietly stalk the fish. But their hasty approach had already sent undulating waves through the water column, alerting the fish that someone or something had entered the pool.

You should realize, too, that any fish that are spooked near you will run forward in the pool to escape, putting every other fish in the pool on the alert — it's sort of a domino effect that warns all the fish that danger is nearby.

APPROACH QUIETLY

Fish can become aware of your approach in several other ways. One indicator is noise or vibrations. Consider that sound travels through water four times more efficiently than through air, and you will realize that noise is something you need to keep in mind when you are executing your approach to any fish.

No Noise on Riverbank

Heavy walking or jumping down along the bank are two examples. On streams that have banks coated in gravel and small stones, a descent down such a bank will usually create a great deal of noise which the fish will probably hear.

While there are circumstances in which soft metal cleats are necessary to keep from slipping and falling when wading, they should be used only when absolutely necessary. Grating of these cleats against the stones on the river bottom is a sure indicator to the fish that a human is coming close. When possible and safe, use only felt-covered soles on your waders or hip boots.

Another factor which I think warns fish of the angler's presence is the use of wading staffs that have metal tips. I know a lot of people use aluminum ski poles. But metal scraping or contacting against rocks makes a loud noise underwater. To avoid this problem, while it will wear out frequently and have to be replaced, I pad the end of my staff with a rubber crutch tip.

Another cardinal rule of approach is that you should never get into the water unless it is necessary. Since water transmits sound so much more efficiently than air, try to stay out of the water. If you are on a bonefish flat and the water is so shallow that the boat can't reach the fish, you will have to get out and wade. On a trout stream overhung with brush, you may have to get into the stream. But, if there is a way to make a cast without getting in the water, always take that option.

In New Zealand, where the trout are big but mighty spooky, guides tell me the two most common mistakes they observe among American anglers is that they rush to get into the water as soon as they reach streamside, and they false cast too much. I suppose that's because a lot of American anglers simply like to wade and false cast a lot. And that may be why many of these anglers are disappointed

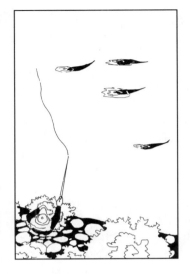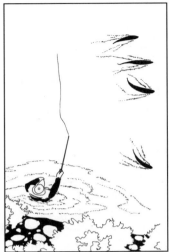

Don't Get in Water

with the results of their long-awaited dream trip to New Zealand. *Only get in the water when you have to.*

Noise can also carry a long distance. Knowledgeable tarpon guides know this, and they won't run a motor within a quarter of a mile of tarpon they know to be resting in a quiet basin. Instead, these guides will shut down their engines and pole. If several guides are working a basin that holds tarpon and one guide decides to leave, a good one will follow the practice of poling more than a quarter of a mile away from the other guides, and only then starting his engine and running it at idle as slowly and quietly as possible as he departs the area.

It always amazes me when I see a modern bass boat roar into a cove, shut off the engine, and with a loud thump drop an electric trolling motor over the side. Then the anglers begin casting as they move along, apparently unaware that the huge wave created by their approach, that first rolled out from the boat and then crashed on the shore, had alerted every bass in the area that someone had definitely arrived. Also, the heavy thumping noise of putting the electric motor into position only confirmed to the fish the existence in the area of a strange presence.

For some years Florida Keys guides used electric motors instead of the more laborious method of poling towards tarpon. I have maintained for years that while the electric motor doesn't necessarily startle fish, it definitely puts them on the alert. Gradually, the better guides in the Keys are beginning to understand that they should use electric motors only when it's absolutely necessary and then, only as little as possible. Even though it's a great deal more work, some of the best guides have gone back to poling exclusively. They report a definite improvement in their fishing success.

When using a boat and entering any quiet cove, extra care should be taken. In the calm of early morning or late evening the roaring of an outboard alerts every fish in a cove that danger is nearby. Instead, cut the engine and either paddle, pole or use an electric motor to make your approach as quietly as possible. Far too many lake fishermen do not consider how noise can effect their fishing.

I believe that loud talking will not alert fish if the water is moving along rapidly, such as in a fast-moving stream, or when the fish are deep in the water column. But when they are in shallow water, I have no doubt that fish can hear loud talking. Sound waves move more easily through water than through air. You can test this for yourself. The next time you are trout fishing, locate a fish holding in a few inches of water at the tail of a smooth, slick pool (or in saltwater, a bonefish swimming in less than a foot of water), and yell loudly. Almost always the fish scoots away. So if you must carry on a conversation with a companion, do it in as low a voice as you can.

A good rule to keep in mind when approaching all fish is that any foreign noise entering their environment is going to alert the fish and make them more difficult to catch. Anytime a fish hears an unusual sound, or sees an abnormal movement, it regards this as a threat and even if it doesn't flee for safety, it has been forewarned to a possible danger and will be more difficult to catch.

APPROACH LOWLY

You can pretty much be assured that any fish that you see can probably see you, especially if you are positioned to its front or side. A cautious approach from behind the fish seems to allow your getting close without it being aware of your presence. So when you sneak up on a fish, accept the assumption that if you're standing up and can see the fish clearly, unless you are directly behind it, it can probably see

Approach Lowly

you, too. But, if you lower your body until you can no longer see the fish, then it probably won't be able to see you either. So once the fish is located, you should make your approach keeping low enough so that you can't see the fish. Only after you have gotten into position to make your cast should you raise your body high enough in order to see your quarry.

APPROACH DARKLY

Carrying any equipment with highly reflective surfaces should be avoided when fishing. For example, some trout fishermen use stainless steel hemostats to remove hooks from fish. And many will attach the hemostats by a chain to a yo-yo gadget, hanging them on their vest, sometimes with a pair of clippers, both of which are silver in color and highly reflective. So any movement by the angler results in these reflective items moving and giving off flashes of light that alert wary fish. If you carry such tools, either keep them concealed while fishing, or paint them a dull color.

The value of approaching darkly also applies to keeping yourself hidden as well as possible. Many years ago, I learned this valuable lesson about approaching trout in a stream from an old hillbilly in the Smoky Mountains of North Carolina. This character was like a fishing vacuum cleaner as he went from pool to pool, hooking trout. Many times he was less than 15 feet away from the fish he caught. He used a technique that I had never given much thought to at that time. He approached fish in the usual way, slowly and with a low profile, but more importantly, he stayed in the shade. He claimed that camouflaging himself by wearing dark clothes and staying in the shade were his greatest assets in catching fish. "It's amazing how much movement you can make and how close you can get, and the trout doesn't seem to notice you," he explained.

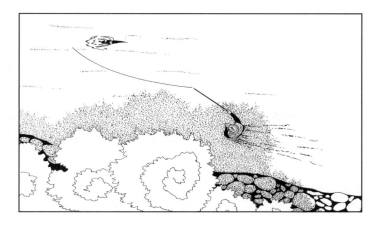

Stay in Shade

His advice is something I have used to great advantage ever since. Whenever it is possible I try to wear dark clothing and make my approach from a shaded portion of the stream.

An added advantage of seeking out shade is that you may also find fish there, as fish lie in the shade whenever possible. After all, the trout is a predator too, and uses the same techniques that a good angler does. So before you move into a shady area, it's advisable to look it over thoroughly for possible fish holding there before you enter it.

APPROACH PATIENTLY

A trout will feed on dry flies for an extraordinarily long time. Rarely does it stop until the hatch is over — or until it has its fill. The problem that I find with many trout fishermen is that they ignore this fact and rush too much. They see a trout, and then without further thought will hastily tie on a fly and begin casting. An experienced angler will stop, sit down, watch, and then watch some more.

If you want to see for yourself how long a trout will continue to rise to dry flies, do this. Find a rising trout and note the time on your watch. Then, sit down, and if you have the patience, continue to observe the trout until it stops rising. How long will it rise? I've seen some trout rise for more than an hour. Certainly 10 or 15 minutes should be expected of almost any trout, unless the hatch is ending.

This experiment will teach you that you really don't have to rush to cast when you see a rising trout. So take your time and carefully plan your approach and presentation. Rushing is a major fault of those inexperienced at dry-fly fishing (the same could be said for nymph fishermen, too). Remember, patiently observe and then plan a good approach and presentation.

PLAN YOUR APPROACH IN ADVANCE

Plan Your Direction

The direction from which you approach a pool can often determine your measure of success.

In the late 1950s, I learned a valuable lesson concerning the direction of approach on a trout stream, a principle which is usually ignored by other anglers. The Letort Spring Run (usually just called the Letort) in Carlisle, Pennsylvania, is one of the most famous and photographed trout streams in American trout angling history. It was on this small spring-fed limestone stream that Charles Fox, Vince Marinaro and Ross Trimmer developed their famous series of terrestrial flies that are now used around the world by trout fishermen. What makes the Letort such a good trout stream is its beds of aquatic vegetation, mostly watercress and *elodea*.

The Letort has an average width of about 40 feet, bordered on its right side (if you are facing upstream) mainly by meadows. The left side holds a number of small marshes created by the springs that ooze up through the ground and flow into the stream, as well as numerous high trees. For obvious reasons, the left side is rarely fished. In fact, during the first four years I fished the Letort, I never saw anyone fish the left side.

Once by chance, in an attempt to get photographs with a fresh perspective for a magazine article I was working on, I decided to go to the left bank and take some shots. It was a most revealing afternoon.

Moving along the left bank, I became aware almost immediately of something odd. Almost all of the larger trout (these were very wise brown trout) were holding in the stream alongside the vegetation on the left side, the side I was on. But all angling traffic was along the right bank of the stream, so the anglers on that side were prevented from seeing most of these trout. And even if they could sight the fish, their chances of executing good casts over the vegetation and achieving a drag-free drift with their flies were severely reduced.

Fish on Opposite Side of Stream

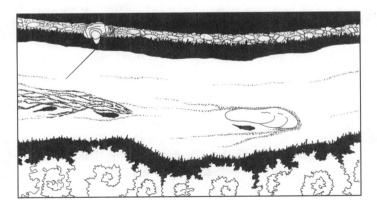

I quickly took the photos I needed for the magazine article and rushed back to the other side and rigged my tackle. After crossing back over and moving upstream, I had the best day of fishing to date that I had ever experienced on the Letort.

Now I must confess that for a long time I never shared this secret with anyone, not because I was selfish (I hope), but because I felt that it gave the trout an edge that might have been taken away if I publicized it.

Benefiting from that experience, I have had good success on many hard-fished trout streams by deliberately working from the bank opposite where most of the angling action was taking place. Now it's almost a commandment with me to fish the opposite bank of a stream if it's obvious that one bank is heavily used by anglers and the other side is being virtually ignored.

Plan Your Position

Getting into the proper position, relative to that of the fish in the water, is vital to a good presentation. It's a principle many anglers don't consider, to their regret.

Position Yourself for the Cast — Proper position means first, that you will be in a place where you can make a good cast. You need to examine your location for any possible obstructions. If one bank is bare with little or no concealing brush, try to avoid coming to the water from that side. If one side of a stream bank has high trees or dense brush as high or even higher than you are, this is likely the best side from which to approach the water, providing you have enough room to make a back cast. Or if there is a large tree standing along the streambank, use it to hide behind as you approach and cast to the fish in the pool. If there is not enough room for a back cast, then you need to approach from a different angle.

If there is a tree overhanging your target area, but one which has an opening between its branches, in order to get the fly under that particular tree for a successful presentation, keep in mind that you will need to consider the space requirements for both your back and forward casts. When throwing to such a confined target, it's usually best to align yourself with the target opening so that your back cast can be delivered in a straight line opposite the target.

When fishing small farm ponds from the bank, a correct position will help in making better presentations. So as you are walking around the pond to locate fish, always have the pond on the same side as your casting hand so that all your back and forward casts will travel over water. Walking in the opposite direction will inevitably place your fly in jeopardy, as it will be traveling along the shoreline over brush and trees upon which it can easily snag.

When fishing in a boat offshore or on a lake, if you spot predator fish feeding on baitfish on the surface of the water, there is also a correct casting position to assume. Pay attention to your line first. The line that you plan to shoot toward the target should not be left lying on the deck where it can blow all over the place during the chase, but in a large bucket. Then — to give you a right-handed example — take a position at the stern of the boat on the starboard (or right) side, facing forward so you can keep your eyes on the fish.

I usually follow the procedure of taking that position, and as my boatman and I are making our run at the fish, stripping off about 30 feet of line and letting it dangle off the rod tip. The speed of the boat will normally keep this much line and the fly aloft as we dash toward the feeding

OVERLEAF: *A typical "line-up" of boats and king salmon anglers on the coastal waters of the northwestern U.S. This one occurred on California's Eel River in late September.*

fish. Upon our arrival at the target area, I will ask the boat-man to turn the bow of the craft slightly to port as he chops the throttle, so that from the starboard side I have a clean shot over water to make my cast and shoot line into the feeding fish.

When fishing from a canoe or small boat on a river or lake, the direction that the craft is moved in relation to the shoreline can make a difference. Assuming the angler is right-handed and sitting in the bow, the boat or canoe should be moved along the left bank so that he can make accurate casts entirely over water, without having to worry about hanging his fly up in brush along the bank, and without being concerned about his fishing companion in the stern being hit or hooked by his fly. If it's possible, start your fishing sequence by having the boat moving in the correct direction before casting. On small lakes, this is simply a matter of whether you start paddling in one direction or the other.

Position Yourself for Fighting and Landing the Fish — But good positioning also means that if the fish takes the fly, you'll be able to continue the fight to a successful conclusion. It does you no good to make a perfect cast, have the fish take your fly, and then be trapped along a streambank, unable to follow the fish. I've occasionally seen people hook large trout at the upstream lip of a rapids bordered by rocks too high for them to climb. In such situations, when the fish is hooked and in its panic swims upstream into the rapids, the angler is unable to follow his line upstream, and a broken leader and a lost fish are the result.

I confess I've made this mistake myself many, many times. I remember one time spotting a terrific cutthroat trout on the Yellowstone River. To cast from the side I was on would have given me a drag problem that I might have had trouble with. But by wading to the other side and climbing down a steep bank, I could make an easy cast with a good drift. Upon doing this, I successfully hooked the fish. But, as soon as it bolted downstream, I was trapped on the cliff, unable to follow, and consequently lost him. This experience strengthened my conviction that you will increase your chances of success if you will plan the various positions which you may have to take in fighting and landing the fish before you make your cast.

Position Yourself for the Proper Fly Presentation — Good positioning also relates to one of the most overlooked tactical principles of fly fishing: in presenting a fly or a streamer to a predatory fish — in fresh or saltwater, the principle is the same for both environments — *a critical consideration is the angle at which the offered fly approaches the fish.* Therefore, in making his approach, the experienced angler will always attempt to place himself at an angle to the fish that will be most favorable to his cast and presentation of the fly.

Since (as we all should know, I suppose) trout almost always face upstream into the current to feed upon food that is drifting downstream to them, when fishing for trout in a stream, most of the time you should plan to position yourself to make an upstream presentation. But in an eddy, trout may face sideways or even downstream to the main flow. So it obviously helps if you can see the fish in order to know in which direction it is facing before you make your presentation. If not, your fly may approach from behind and flush your quarry.

There are many tactical situations on streams that require that the fly approach the fish from a specific direction, which may not necessarily be from downstream. Steelheaders and Atlantic salmon fishermen soon learn this. But this technique often applies to other freshwater species as well. Smallmouth bass, for example, will often hold in very definite locations, usually near a rock or rock ledge.

In these situations, to get the fly moving properly towards the fish means that the angler needs to position himself quite precisely. A violation of this principle generally results in the angler delivering a poorly presented fly that will be refused by the fish.

When approaching a trout pool, the angler can almost always count on the fact that most of the fish will be either in the upper or lower end of the pool below a riffle — especially if they are feeding. The riffle is the grocery shelf where most of the trout's aquatic foods live. Nymphs, crayfish, hellgrammites and other morsels live among or under the rock rubble of a riffle. As these bait species move around, they are frequently swept into the current and carried into the pool. Trout know this and will hold just below the riffle, awaiting the food that drifts to them.

Trout may also hold at the very bottom of a pool, which usually has one to three narrow channels where the current is constricted, forcing most of the food traveling from the

Where Trout Hold in Pool

head of the pool to drift through these channels down through the bottom of the pool. Feeding trout will frequently lie in such channels so that as the food is funneled through they can swallow it without having to move very far or expend much energy.

Position Yourself for Safety — For reasons of safety, positioning is also important when fly fishing from a boat. If you are being poled across a flat for bonefish, tarpon, permit, or other shallow saltwater species, you should make it a firm rule never to cast directly in front of the boat. Remember, the person poling the boat is directly behind you. Since your back and forward casts must travel in the same plane, the chances of hooking your friend (at least he was until you began casting) on casts aimed directly forward of the boat are very real.

When a fish is spotted, wait until your companion handling the boat can swing the rear of the boat around to an angle from the fish at which you can safely cast.

For example, if you are moving due north and see a fish approaching, don't cast immediately. Allow the boatman to sweep the boat at right angles to you (to the east or west

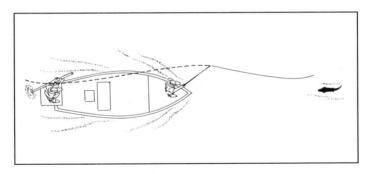

Incorrect Boat Casting Position

depending upon whether you are a right or left-handed caster) in order to position the rear of the boat to the side opposite your rod hand. This will allow you to cast back and

45

forth over the water without any chance of hooking your companion.

Whether you are on foot or in a boat, it pays to preplan all of your positioning tactics before you make your presentation. And for a number of reasons we have discussed, assuming a position so that you can make unimpeded casts to the fish, generally on an angle, is recommended.

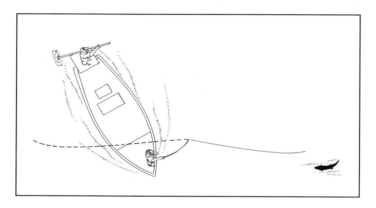

Correct Boat Casting Position

TIPS ON SALTWATER APPROACHES

In saltwater it is important to understand tides, and what effect they have on both predator fish and their prey. Perhaps the single most important thing to realize is that the various saltwater prey species (crabs, small baitfish, shrimp, etc.) do not have a permanent home site, as do minnows in a freshwater stream. Minnows in freshwater environments live in a "home pool." They were born in this pool, and they will try to remain in it throughout their lives. Should rains raise the water to flood stage, minnows will seek shelter under a rock or log along the streambank, making every effort not to be swept out of "their" pool.

This is not the case in saltwater. Saltwater prey species are born in the open sea, and never have a permanent home. They go where the tide takes them, and are therefore keenly aware of tidal action and its implications for their existence. It would be foolish for a mullet caught in a swift tidal current to attempt to remain in such a flow. As tough as its life is anyway, it would be wasting energy that could be better devoted to more important activities, like staying alive, for instance. The baitfish prey for saltwater species are always going to go where the tide takes them ... you might say "they go with the flow."

In most areas of the world there are two high and two low tides each day. Roughly every six hours the tide changes. Keeping this in mind, as you examine the area you are intending to fish, you can devise a tactical approach that will increase your chances for success.

Most bonefish (and many other saltwater species) will work into the tide. The tidal flow carries the scent of their prey to them. Anyone who has ever chummed with cut-up shrimp for bonefish can attest that bonefish can smell the chum from as far down current as a 100 yards — perhaps even more.

At low tide, when the tidal flat is nearly dry, crabs and other creatures are safe from bonefish. But as the tide rises, bonefish can approach these creatures. And they will attempt to do so by swimming into the current.

Therefore, a classic place to fly fish in saltwater is where there is a basin or bay with a narrow opening through which the tide has to flow to fill and drain the basin or bay. In these places, the direction from which you approach and make your casts will be the major determining factor as to whether or not you catch many fish.

As the incoming tide flows into a bay, the current rushes through the opening, carrying with it any creatures that are

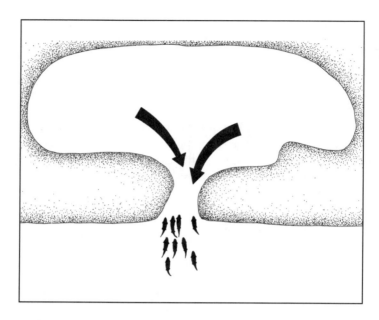

Fish the Mouth of the Funnel

being forced by the tide to take them wherever it goes. What you want to do is approach quietly and anchor on the inside of the bay, where the water flows through the funnel-like channel. Later, when the tide begins to fall and the water is now being funneled out of the bay, motor to the outside of the bay's opening and anchor. Then you can get a shot at anything that flows out of the mouth of the funnel.

Another tactic in saltwater fly fishing is to recognize underwater points — generally low obstructions of rock, sand or coral that have built up over time through tidal action

Kathi Delzer with a monster bluegill — over two pounds! — caught while fly fishing from a tube on Barnes Butte Lake, central Oregon. ➤

just below the surface of the water — and their importance to the angler. Professional bass fishermen are keenly aware of the importance of underwater points in freshwater angling, but it is a factor that is generally overlooked by saltwater anglers.

Let me explain. As fish swim along they position themselves in relatively deep water (it may be two feet for bonefish, three feet for permit, and as much as 11 feet or more for tarpon). If there is a shallow point of rock, sand, or coral extending out into the path the fish are following, they will usually go around it. By carefully approaching such underwater points, and then anchoring, you can wait and see approaching fish. This is a standard practice with successful tarpon and permit fishermen.

On a saltwater flat, whenever possible try to approach with the sun behind you, or at least at an angle behind you. If you make your approach directly into the sun you will be confronted with total glare on the water. When fishing for tarpon, snook, bonefish, redfish and permit, you need to see the target before you can make your approach and cast. With the sun directly behind you there is little glare on the water, and only a little more if the sun is to your side. Or when there is a white cloud in the foreground, all you will see is white glare from the cloud, making visibility under the surface impossible. To avoid such glare problems, you may have to move a considerable distance to set up your approach from another angle.

When you are fishing from a boat and spot a cruising fish, a well planned approach will certainly help. For example, what appears to be a shark slowly moving across the flat with that distinctive wig-wag motion of its tail, is not really such a slow-moving creature at all. Instead the shark is probably moving at a surprisingly rapid pace. Trying to pole after the average cruising shark or tarpon is almost a futile experience. In these circumstances, you will have to plan your approach differently, if that is possible.

Sometimes you can allow such a fish to get a little distance from you and then pole to the nearest deep water. Note the direction that the shark or tarpon is swimming. Then motor well ahead in that direction, shut down the motor and pole toward the fish to intercept it.

BASIC RULES FOR APPROACHING FISH

1. In approaching any fish, you should make your approach so that the fish is never aware that you are there.
2. Only wade when you have to.
3. False cast as little as possible.
4. Approach slowly.
5. Approach quietly.
6. Approach lowly.
7. Approach darkly.
8. Approach patiently.
9. Plan the direction of your approach and casting position in advance.
10. In saltwater ...
    ... understand tidal action;
    ... understand underwater points;
    ... understand sun position.

OVERLEAF: *Jim Teeny with his world's record sockeye salmon, caught on the Brooks River, Alaska. Chapter Three examines the selection of sinking lines, followed in Chapter Four by a discussion of underwater fly presentation and retrieving tactics.*

FLY LINE, LEADER, TIPPET AND FLY SELECTION

Let's first discuss tackle as it relates to presentation and retrieving technique. And that really means focusing on the components of fly-fishing tackle that are the fundamental instruments of presentation and retrieving: lines, leaders, tippets, and flies.

FLY LINE SELECTION

In most fly-fishing situations, an essential factor for successful presentations is the fly line that you use. A presentation with an incorrect line makes effective retrieving and hook-ups very difficult. Use the right line and things are so easy. Proper line selection is based upon two criteria: *the size of the line* and *its design performance in the water*, that is, its *type*, as defined by its floating or sinking characteristics.

One well known rule of line selection is that the size of the fly determines the size of the line. In other words, *big fly equals big line.* What's less well understood by many anglers, however, are the design performance characteristics of the various types of fly lines that are available today, and when and where each type of line should be used.

Many anglers fly fish their whole lives using only a floating fly line. That's okay, I suppose. But they won't catch all the fish that they should, as there are really a large number of situations in which another type of line — sinking-tip, slow-sinking, fast-sinking, or shooting-taper — will deliver a better presentation and increase fishing success. So after reviewing presentations with floating lines, we'll examine the other line options that are now available to you.

Presentations with Floating Lines

In calm water situations the angler should use the lightest floating fly line that will deliver the fly. For dry-fly fishing to freshwater species, only rarely is a size 6 or heavier line needed. Most of the time, a 2, 3, or 4-weight line is best for dry-fly fishing. Such light lines settle to the water almost silently. Unless it is very windy, the angler using dry flies will simply catch more fish if he uses lines of size 2, 3 or 4 most of the time.

When conditions are windy, a different line selection should be made, based upon the distance needed for the cast. If you are fishing at short distances (less than 25 to 30 feet), *use a line one size larger*. This allows you to load the rod with only a short amount of fly line outside the rod tip.

But if you are going to cast into the wind at long distances, *then use a line one size smaller, with at least 40 feet of line extended beyond the rod tip for false casting*. This amount of extended line will allow you to load the lighter-weight line properly, and of course, because you are false casting a considerable length of line, your fly will be closer to the target when you finally release the line.

Don't do the reverse: don't use a heavier line than normal when attempting to false cast a lot of line in heavy wind, as this will cause your rod to bow deeply, creating large, open loops that won't drive well into a breeze.

Light floating lines should also be used on very calm days in saltwater. I opt for a size 6 line for bonefishing. Such lines come to the water so softly that I can cast with a 10-foot leader to even very shy fish.

But this light line principle also applies to saltwater species other than nervous bonefish. The shark, a species that lately has become increasingly popular with saltwater fly fishermen, may seem a primitive and unemotional creature, but in low clear water a shark can be very easily alarmed. A heavy size 12 or 13 line crashing to the surface on a calm day will spook a shark just as easily as it would a bonefish. In such situations, a size 9 or 10 line would be much preferred.

When fishing for tarpon on a dead calm day, a size 10 line that falls to the water relatively quietly gives the angler a much better chance than a heavy 12 to 14 size line clunking down to the surface.

Tarpon are often spooked by the line following immediately behind the leader. A clear monofilament fly line (or shooting head of clear monofilament) is far less likely to spook fish. This is especially true when fishing for tarpon over a light, sandy bottom.

For that reason, one of my favorite fly lines for fishing tarpon is sold by Orvis (address: 10 River Road, Manchester, Vermont 05254; telephone 800-548-9548). This is a floating line which has the front portion constructed of 10 feet of clear monofilament. There are two very desirable characteristics to this line.

When it's combined with a six to 10-foot leader, you then have 16 to 20 feet of transparent line behind the fly, a length that reduces the chances of the fish seeing the line.

Its other characteristic, which I especially like, is that since the rear portion of the line floats, you can make the cast in front of a school of approaching tarpon, then wait while you hold the fly suspended in the water column as the fish approach. When the fish reach the position that you think is just right, begin your retrieve.

Or on those occasions when you have offered the fly to one tarpon and it swims by without interest, the retrieve can be stopped while the floating portion of the line holds the fly suspended in the water column. When the next tarpon swims into position, you can begin retrieving again.

Redfish are often maligned as having poor eyesight (an observation I don't necessarily agree with), but these wily fish certainly have keen hearing. So when possible, go no heavier than a 7 or 8-weight line on redfish, and only resort to 9 and 10 weights when fishing conditions demand these heavier lines.

Under calm conditions, make it a firm rule to use the lightest floating line possible and you will up your score considerably on most species in both fresh and saltwater.

Presentations with Sinking-Tip Lines

With the exception of trout fishing, sinking-tip lines are not good lines for most fishing situations. Of all fly lines, sinking-tip lines are the most difficult to cast and make a quiet presentation with. And with a sinking-tip line, every time you strip in some line, you cause the forward portion of the line which is already submerged to loft toward the surface, pulling the fly away from your intended course of travel. If your tactic requires that the fly line travel at the same uniform depth throughout the water column, you need to use another type of sinking line, not a sinking-tip.

There is one situation, however, in which the sinking-tip line is the perfect presentation tool: whenever you have to cast into a small open hole in vegetation, retrieve the line across the vegetation, and then make a back cast. This frequently occurs in fishing for largemouth bass in water where the surface is choked with lily pads; or when attempting to get to a snook lying in a pothole on a saltwater flat. In such situations, a floating line cannot be used successfully because it won't drive the fly as deeply into the water as is required. But a sinking-tip works very well, in the following typical routine: the cast is made and the fly is dropped on the far side of the hole ... you allow the fly to sink into the depths of the hole and then begin your retrieve ... when the fly nears the edge of the hole, you make a back cast. In this situation, the long, rear floating portion of the sinking-tip line permits an easy back cast to be made; whereas a full-sinking line would tangle in the lily pads or grass as you attempt the back cast.

Presentations with Slow-Sinking Lines

Five types of full-sinking fly lines are in general manufacture today. They are distinguished from each other by their sink rate in the water column, from slow-sinking to extra-fast-sinking.

Let's look at the slow-sinking line first.

In saltwater, the water that you want to fish is often filled with floating grass, sometimes so thick as to make fishing nearly impossible. At other times, often during the first few days after extra-high tidal conditions, the abnormally high water carries small pieces of grass and deposits them along shorelines and over the surface of the water of the areas you wish to fish.

A floating line is useless in these situations; it will simply lie on top of the grass carpeting the surface until you begin the retrieve, at which time the grass slides down the floating line, then over the leader and onto your fly, ruining your retrieve.

A slow-sinking line — often called an intermediate line — is an ideal choice for a situation such as this, when the fish are not too deep in the water column and you need to keep your fly tracking towards the surface.

When you cast a slow-sinking line onto pieces of floating grass, it will slowly slide off to one side of the bothersome grass and descend an inch or two below the surface of the water, remaining in that position a fair amount of time before you will want to begin your retrieve. Such a line gives you the advantage of being able to present your fly near the surface of the water, while eliminating the problems associated with grass.

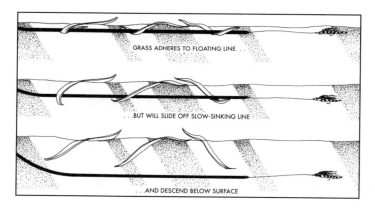

GRASS ADHERES TO FLOATING LINE...

...BUT WILL SLIDE OFF SLOW-SINKING LINE

...AND DESCEND BELOW SURFACE

Slow-Sinking Line in Grass

Another common use for slow-sinking lines is in Atlantic salmon fishing with tube flies, which apparently are most effective when they are fished just below the surface of the water on the swing.

Presentations with Fast-Sinking Lines

All sinking lines need to be evaluated based upon how rapidly, how deeply, and how effectively they sink into the water column.

Years ago, when I was doing the research for the first edition of my book, *Fly Fishing in Salt Water*, I asked a number of experts if a size 8 fast-sinking fly line would sink faster than the same type line in size 10. No one seemed to know. I conducted several simple experiments and soon determined that the size 10 line would sink much faster, confirming my belief that the heavier the sinking line, the faster it will sink.

You can therefore conclude that how fast and how deep you want the fly to sink will depend either upon selecting a larger size sinking line, or one that has a faster sink rate. But more than anything, the important consideration about a sinking line is *how well it sinks to the depth in the water column that you perceive the fish to be in, and therefore where you want to position your fly.*

In that important regard, conventional sinking lines are simply not a good presentation instrument, and I do not recommend them, except in special situations.

That basis of the flaw in most commercially manufactured conventional sinking lines is that the front section of the line — about the first 10 feet or so — has been deliberately designed to taper in order to achieve better turnover of the leader and fly on the cast. This means, therefore, that in a conventional sinking line, the front 10 feet or so will weigh less than the mid-section of the line (the belly), and thus it will not sink as rapidly, which, in turn, creates an underwater bow in the line. As the angler fishes this type line at a depth in the water column that he perceives fish to be holding, while the belly of the line may sink fast and deep enough to reach the fish, the front section of the line, including the leader and fly, has bowed up and is riding

OVERLEAF: *Gris Bettle with a bonefish hook-up, Ascension Bay, Yucatan, Mexico.*

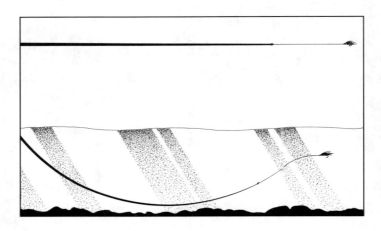

Profile of Conventional Sinking Line

higher in the water column than the angler perceived the fish to be. That's not a good way to catch fish.

Fortunately, there's a way to overcome this deficiency, with a uniform-sinking line or one of the weights in the T-Series of Teeny Nymph Lines.

Uniform-sinking lines have almost a straight taper to the forward segment, which is weighted to conform to, and have the general casting characteristics of, a conventional weight-forward floating line. These lines are readily available from most all of the large fly line manufacturers, and can be purchased in five different sink rates from slow-sinking to extra fast-sinking.

The T-Series of Teeny Lines are constructed with a sinking belly section joined to a variety of head sections in five weights, designated as T-130, T-200, T-300, T-400 and T-500. The numbers indicate the grain weight, and thus the sinking rate, of the head section of the line, which for the T-130, T-200, T-300 and T-400 models is 24 feet long, and for the T-500 model is 28 feet long. For example, a popular

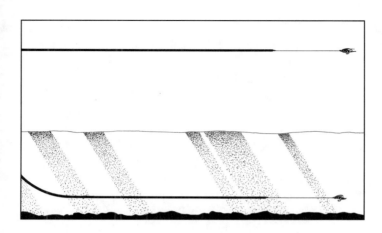

Profile of Uniform-Sinking and Teeny Nymph Lines

model designed to work well with a 7 or 8-weight rod, the T-200, has a head section 24 feet long weighing 200 grains. I understand that Teeny lines are now available in many fly shops, or you may obtain more information directly from the Jim Teeny Incorporated (address: P.O. Box 989, Gresham, Oregon 97030; telephone 503-667-6602).

There are several other advantages in using uniform-sinking and Teeny Nymph Lines. One of their principal advantages is that you feel the presence of the fish on your fly faster and better, whether it's the delicate inhalation of a nymph, or a slam dunk on a big streamer pattern. This is because instead of having the underwater bow in the line, which is created by the conventional sinking line, uniform-sinking and Teeny Nymph lines travel straight through the water. Thus when a fish makes contact with the fly, you are immediately aware of it.

This same factor aids in striking more efficiently. Striking with a conventional sinking line means that you have to get rid of the slack, or the bow, in the forward end of the line and leader before you can stick the fish. With the uniform-sinking and Teeny Nymph lines, which travel straight at the fish, all you have to do is strike and the hook starts to bury itself in the fish's mouth immediately.

Yet another advantage I have found with these lines is their effectiveness in casting in strong winds. Fishing for sea-run brown trout in Tierra del Fuego, Argentina, we were often casting flies in winds that exceeded 30 mph — and would you believe one day it was blowing 50 mph? It soon became apparent that if a good cast was to be made, there had to be a lot of weight in the forward portion of the line. The uniform-sinking and Teeny Nymph lines, with no taper and more weight forward, tended to buck the breeze and turn the fly over so much better than a conventional sinking line with its tapered and thinner front portion.

In offshore saltwater fishing, while floating lines have a small niche for specialized applications, perhaps 90 percent of all offshore fishing is best practiced with sinking lines, as most offshore species — dolphin, wahoo, and all types of billfish — normally swim at some depth below the surface of the ocean. A slow-sinking and a fast-sinking line are the two mainstays for these type presentations So if you are stuck with only one line for offshore fly fishing — go for the faster sinking line and adjust your retrieve. Or in the alternative, you may elect to use a sinking shooting head, as I will discuss below.

Presentations with Shooting Heads

We now know that there are many fishing circumstances when the shooting head is the best tool available for presenting the fly to the fish.

"Shooting taper" is the generic term for this type of fly line. But the term "shooting head" (which was first adopted by one of our major fly line manufacturers. Scientific Anglers) is now the term commonly used by most anglers to describe this type of specialized fly line. However, most manufacturers continue to refer to the line as a "shooting taper," and thus the technical designation that generally appears on retail cartons for shooting heads is "ST." For example, a 9-weight floating shooting head would be indicated on the carton as ST9F. This means: shooting taper — number 9 line — floating. But I prefer to follow the common usage.

The first anglers to regularly employ shooting heads were steelhead fly fishermen on the big rivers of the Northwest, where more often than not, the premium holding pockets for steelhead were far out in the stream beyond stretches of water that were too deep for wading. The shooting head allowed the anglers to reach these pockets with extremely long casts.

We have since learned over the years that the shooting head is essential for many types of presentations in both fresh and saltwater. And I think that any serious fly fisherman is missing a great fly-fishing experience, and missing out on a lot of big fish, if he does not learn to construct, work with, and cast shooting heads.

Anytime you want to present a fly at a long distance through the water, the shooting head is a superior tool. And in those situations when you want to sink your fly down deep in the water column, no line matches the effectiveness of a fast-sinking shooting head (or lead-core line made into a shooting head).

A shooting head is identical to the forward portion of a conventional weight-forward or double-taper fly line, and may be purchased commercially as an individual item or constructed by cutting one out of a conventional line — although those made from double-taper lines seem to cast a little better. When it is rigged, the forward part of the line

— the *shooting head* — will be attached to an extra-thin rear segment, called the *shooting line*.

When you are fishing, the shooting head is held outside the rod tip while false casting. On the last forward cast, as the rod stops, the thinner (shooting) line to the rear is released. Because the skinny shooting line offers almost no resistance, the heavier, fast-traveling shooting head easily pulls a lot of the shooting line toward the target. One of the great attributes of this line is that it allows you to work and search a fly through considerably more water than you could with another type of line. And no fly line permits the angler to make longer casts than the shooting head.

When shooting heads were first sold, the manufacturers made them 30 feet long, as traditionally this was the length they had always agreed upon as being the standard for measuring the weight designation of conventional fly lines. Thus, the first 30 feet of a line that's designated as number 6 weighs about 160 grains, while the first 30 feet of a line that's designated as number 10 weighs about 280 grains, and so on. Manufacturers continue to use these designations for conventional fly lines today, so that when they began manufacturing shooting heads, it seemed to them a reasonable idea also to make shooting heads 30 feet long so that their weight could be similarly measured and designated in the same manner.

But there is a problem with this. One of the most important facts to understand about distance casting is that as soon as the line unrolls (or straightens) it will begin falling. *Only so long as the line is unrolling in the air, does it travel toward the target.* If a commercial shooting head is 30 feet long, then no matter what the skill of the caster, as soon as that 30 feet unrolls, it will begin falling to the water. Make the head longer and you increase the unroll time — and the distance that you can cast the fly.

So instead of purchasing commercial shooting heads, I suggest that you make your own shooting heads that will provide you with greater distance on your cast than those sold commercially.

They are very easy to make. Buy a double-taper fly line *one size larger* than you need for the rod. For example, if you are casting with an 8-weight rod, then buy a number 9 double-taper line.

A double-taper line has a long level section in the middle of the line with identical tapers at each end. Thus from a single double-taper line you can make two shooting heads. If you purchase a weight-forward line for this purpose, you're wasting your money, because you can only get one shooting taper from it, since the rear portion of this line is not weighted and tapered, but is very long and thin.

The length of the shooting head you construct will be determined by your casting skill. A very good caster can effortlessly handle a shooting head from about 38 to 40 feet long. Anglers who can cast easily to about 60 feet seem to be able to handle a shooting head of 34 or 35 feet in length. The best way to determine what is right for you is to construct a head to the maximum length that you believe you can handle and try it out. If you find that it's a little too long for you, simply cut it back and make it shorter. Your testing guideline should be that *the correct length of shooting head for you is the length you can hold outside the rod tip and false cast comfortably.*

Shooting Lines — A number of materials can be used for the shooting line. The one most commonly used is monofilament. Monofilament allows the angler the greatest distance on the shoot, since it is so thin, light and slick.

When fishing with the lighter fly lines, such as 5 through 7 weights, a 20-pound monofilament shooting line seems to be the best choice. It does blow around and it will sometimes tangle, but its ability to glide so easily through the guides makes it the first choice when light lines are being thrown any distance.

For heavier lines and when fishing for strong fish — salmon, steelhead, striped bass, tarpon, and other saltwater species, for example — 30-pound shooting line is the universal choice of most experienced anglers.

Monofilament shooting line is best, too, if the angler is really trying to get down deep. It offers the least resistance against the water of any of the materials that are commonly used for shooting lines.

Of all the monofilament lines that I have used, Amnesia monofilament seems to be one of the best, because when you stretch the line, all its coils are immediately removed (Amnesia is manufactured by Sunset Line and Twine Company, P.O. Box 691, Petaluma, California 94953; telephone 707-762-2704).

Some anglers prefer a shooting line made from braided leader material (a line with a hollow core and a braided exterior). The braided shooting line has two outstanding advantages. First, when it is stripped from the spool it falls loosely, with no coiling. The braiding prevents coiling, a problem with all other types of shooting line. (Other kinds can have their coils removed, of course, by stretching them before you start fishing.) And second, the braided line shoots extremely well through the guides.

The disadvantage of braided shooting line is that the material is very rough, and after lengthy periods of fishing, the rough texture of the line can cut right through the skin of your fingers as you grip the line when retrieving.

Commercial braided shooting line is now being manufactured by at least two companies, Cortland Line Company (address: P.O. Box 5588, Cortland, New York 13045; telephone 607-756-2851) and 3M/Scientific Anglers (address: 225-3N-04, 3M Center, St. Paul, Minnesota 55144; telephone 800-525-6290). This product is essentially a size 2 or 3 level fly line with a conventional braided-core body, over which has been applied standard floating fly line material. The size 2 line has a breaking strength of somewhere near 15 to 20 pounds. The size 3 line, which has a diameter of approximately .035, breaks at about 30 pounds, or slightly higher. Obviously, if you are after big gamefish, you will want to use the .035-diameter line. But when you use this weight, be sure that you don't use a leader that is stronger than the shooting line. If you do, and the fish really pulls on the outfit, the shooting line will break and you could lose everything.

Convenience is another good reason for using shooting heads, as they allow for quick and easy loop-to-loop line changes to accommodate any change in the tactical fishing situation that you may encounter at streamside. Simply construct a loop at the rear of each of your various types of shooting heads — floating, slow-sinking, fast-sinking, etc. — and similarly construct a loop at the forward end of your shooting line. This gives you a convenient loop-to-loop system for quick line connects and disconnects. In this manner, you can adjust to any changes in the fishing situation throughout the day with only having to carry just one reel on your rod, plus spare spools loaded with other types of shooting heads in your fishing vest.

A simple method of making a loop for both the shooting head and shooting line is to use a fly tying bobbin and size A tying thread. Follow the directions in the following illustrations. And when making your loop-to-loop connection, always do so in a square knot configuration (also shown), never in the bowline configuration that will weaken the connection and form a large bump that may become jammed on the rod guides.

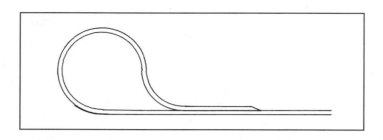

STEP 1   *Use a fly-tying bobbin with size-A thread (Nymo, flat waxed, Kevlar, or any quality thread). Insert the thread through the tube of the bobbin as you normally would. Then, remove the spool and wrap the thread around one of the bobbin legs four times before reseating the spool. The four turns will give you the tension necessary to swing the bobbin with force. If you need more thread, you will have to rotate the spool with your hands to feed the additional amount. To start, fold the fly line back on itself for about two inches to form a loop.*

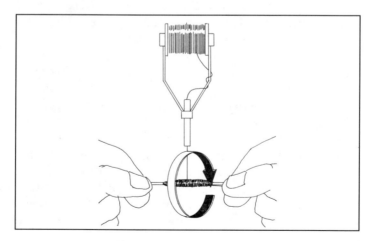

STEP 2   *Lay the tag end of the thread parallel to the tag end of the fly line and make a few turns by hand to secure the loop.*

Grip the loop in your right hand and the fly line (both standing part and tag end) in your left hand. Rotate your hands away from your body to swing the bobbin. The faster you spin it, the deeper the thread will bury itself in the outer coating of the fly line. With practice, you can lay each wrap against the preceding one.

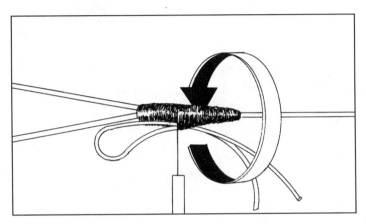

STEP 3   A wrap of 1/2 inch is adequate, but you might want to stretch it to 5/8 or 3/4 of an inch. Stop before you reach that distance, and taper the tag end of the fly line with a sharp knife or razor. This will help to make a smooth transition as you wrap over it down to the single strand of fly line. To secure the wraps so they don't unravel, use a whip-finish. Many anglers prefer to lay a 10-inch piece of doubled mono with the loop in the direction the wraps are going. Mono testing four to 10 pounds is adequate. Make eight or 10 wraps by swinging the bobbin gently. If you swing it too hard, you won't be able to pull the mono back out.

STEP 4   Cut the thread coming from the bobbin and slip the tag end through the loop of monofilament. Hold the fly line

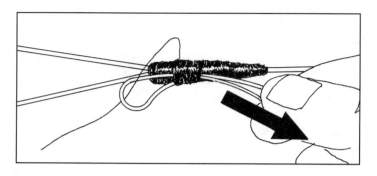

and pull both tag ends of the monofilament at the same time. This will draw the thread under the wraps and secure it.

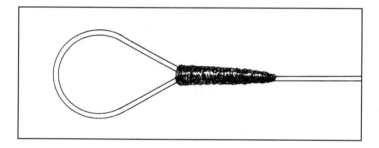

STEP 5   *Trim the thread at the point where it exits the wraps. Then coat the wraps with a glue or rubber-based cement such as Pliobond. Take a moment to test the loop. Place a smooth object in the loop and pull on it with one hand while holding the fly line in the other. If the thread did not bury itself deeply* **enough, the loop will come out.** (Reprinted from *Practical Fishing Knots,* © 1991 by Mark Sosin and Lefty Kreh.)

What type of shooting line is best? It is a personal choice matter, I suppose. But, for most people in most fly-fishing situations, I recommend the commercial shooting line. It shoots well, handles nicely, and is relatively inexpensive.

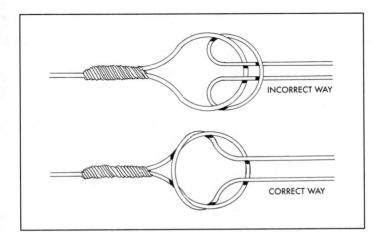

Interlocking Loops

Shooting-Head Tactics — So with your shooting head in hand, let's talk about its use in a few tactical situations. You'll see why I think shooting heads are great. And they're not just for the experts either!

If you are a bass fisherman, fishing smallmouths on a wide river such as the Susquehanna ... or maybe you enjoy fishing surface feeding trout on a calm lake ... or perhaps you are casting to sea trout in a saltwater basin ... or you are fishing a farm pond and need to get the fly well out from the bank ... in these and many more day-to-day fly-fishing situations, if you are only an average or below-average fly caster, when you need to cast a longer distance than you could normally achieve with a weight-forward line, this is where a shooting head can be very helpful.

For offshore fishing, while many anglers prefer to use a conventional fast-sinking line, in most situations I prefer the shooting head. This is primarily because I *never* seem to be able to cast far enough offshore, unless the fish have been teased to the boat. Shooting heads are by far the best choice for offshore long distance casting, at least for me. And to drive the fly deep into the saltwater column, the very best shooting head for me is an extra-fast-sinking (or lead-core) shooting head attached to 25 or 30-pound monofilament. No line goes down faster and has less resistance against the current flow than this type of shooting head/shooting line combination.

For the fly fisherman who is not a particularly good caster and needs a little extra distance — to drop the fly to 45 to 60 feet away, for instance — you can make a *modified shooting head* that works well. I often use this type line when I take someone fishing who has only tried for trout on small streams, or is simply very small or weak — children from 12 to 16 who are not large or strong for their age or elderly persons, for example.

To construct this line, build a shooting head of only 25 feet instead of the commercial 30-foot length. (But remember, make it one size heavier than the rod calls for.) Use 30-pound monofilament for the shooting line. You'll be amazed at how well even weak or very inexperienced anglers can fish with this outfit! I assure you that anybody that can handle a fly rod at all can easily lift a 25-foot shooting head from the water. With this outfit they can lift the 25 feet of shooting head, make a back cast, come forward, and at the end of the forward cast, simply let the shooting line go. This allows them to cast the fly easily to a distance of 45 to 60 feet.

The Effect of Fly Line Color On Presentations

The color of fly lines is a personal choice and many people feel strongly about this. In New Zealand, where the water is as clear as the air, a dull-colored line is often desirable. However, in almost all other fishing situations I have found that line color is not a detriment, at least as regards to its being perceived by fish. In most cases, I believe that if the fish sees the line, it's probably the result of a poor presentation by the angler, not the fly line color. Which brings me to this very important principle:

One of the cardinal rules of presentation is that the fly line should never be thrown over or beyond the fish.

Also, when casting in very clear water, it's often desirable to cast on a side angle, rather than an overhead throw, which simply gives the fish a better chance of seeing the line than you ought to give him.

Where accuracy of presentation is important, a brightly colored line is to be preferred. If you are a fairly good or advanced caster, you will have learned to control your cast well, and a bright color in the line allows you to see it unrolling in the air toward the target. That's a real plus, in my view. I feel that being able to watch the line travel toward the target aids considerably in getting an accurate cast, mainly because if you can see the line, you can slow or stop it when you feel it is the correct moment to do so.

Moreover, the advantage of being able to see brightly colored lines is a help in certain fishing situations. For example, when bass fishing a shoreline early or late in the day when visibility is low, a brightly colored line can help the angler stay in contact with his fly or popping bug. Or when bonefishing or seeking permit, a brightly colored line is preferred simply because it's important to know where the line is so that you can easily relate to the location of the fly.

But there are some rare occasions when a brightly colored line can be detrimental to your presentation technique. If you work a bright line through or close to a school of fish, they will probably flare from it. Generally this occurs in clear water in situations in which the line must be dragged in front of the fish.

And fly fishing for tarpon is an example of where a brightly colored line is often detrimental. That is why so many good tarpon fishermen use a line constructed with the front section composed of clear, or almost clear, monofilament.

But, I think that as a general rule, for me at least, when using a floating fly line in shallow water (less than five feet deep) a brightly colored line is the best choice.

LEADER SELECTION

Presentations with Long Leaders

Long tapered leaders are most often preferred for making a good presentation with a floating line.

Most experienced trout fishermen have long recognized that the more wary the trout, and the calmer the water, the longer the leader needed. This is a presentation rule that is almost absolute. For it is not necessarily the size of the tippet (the end portion of the leader that is the weakest or thinnest) that determines what length leader should be used, but rather the amount of impact the fly line and leader make on the surface of the water; as a heavy leader splash will disturb or alert the trout, reducing the chances of a take. By extending the leader, the angler is able to present his line well away from a wary trout.

On spring creeks, calm lake surfaces, beaver ponds, and when fish are in low, slow-moving, shallow water, a leader at least 12 feet long is desirable. Frequently, a 16-foot leader is not out of the question.

Long leaders also work extremely well when a dry fly needs to be presented downstream. In tactical situations where a cast from downstream of the trout is nearly impossible, often the angler can instead drift his fly downstream to the trout. For this type presentation, a long leader will give a better drag-free drift than a short one. For such presentations I often use a leader that is at least 14 feet or more in length.

Another trout fishing situation where I find that a long leader works extremely well is in skating a fly. I believe this is one of the most exciting and fun-filled ways to catch a trout on the surface. Here's how to go about it.

Locate yourself upstream of a good position for a holding trout. You will need some flowing water, and within limits, the faster the water flow, the better. I coat or dress the leader within a foot of the fly, applying a liberal coating of paste floatant. I also dress the fly very well. This is one time, too, when a long rod — at least nine feet or longer — works best.

Cast the fly downstream, far enough to place it slightly to one side of where you think the trout is holding in the current. Lean the rod to one side. The current pushing against the fly line, and then the leader, will sweep the fly across in front of the holding spot. If there is no take, lean the rod the other way. This will cause the fly to reverse

Fly Skating Technique

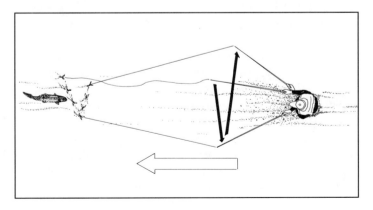

direction and come sweeping back across the target area. By alternating the angle of the rod and switching back and forth in this manner, you can make a fly literally skate along the surface of the water in front of the fish. Many times, this motion is simply too much of a temptation for a hungry trout to ignore.

While this technique can be practiced with a leader of standard length, say eight to nine feet, a longer leader, when dressed properly so that it floats well, will work better to keep the fly on the surface, thus creating a more realistic presentation.

In fishing for trout with imitations that represent tiny chironomids, in which the angler is attempting to imitate their vertical ascent from the lake floor to the surface to exit and hatch, a super-long leader is required.

The proper rig for chironomid presentations is a well-dressed floating line with a 25-foot leader, ending in a light tippet to which is tied the tiny imitation. Proper presentation and retrieve technique is to make a long cast and give the little fly plenty of time to sink as deeply as possible. Then, in a very, very slow retrieve, the fly should be brought back in a vertical ascent. If the fly is down deep, as the line floats the long leader allows it to be brought back in a vertical plane — imitating the ascent of a chironomid.

For steelhead and Atlantic salmon, longer leaders are also necessary when the fish are holding in very shallow water and are especially spooky. Leaders 13 to 15 feet in length with small flies are often just the ticket.

When Pacific salmon move into the estuaries, or even a little farther up the rivers, they will often hold in densely packed schools. It is often necessary to throw the fly slightly up-current and beyond the school, allowing it to sink to the salmon's depth before retrieving. In this case leaders as long as 15 or 16 feet are often employed.

For redfish, a leader from seven to nine feet long is usually fine. But I've seen periods when on dead calm days, where water is as slick as oil-covered glass, that leaders as long as 12 or 13 feet in length, fished with small flies that reduce surface impact, are essential to success.

Other saltwater situations in which long leader presentations should be adopted is when making delicate casts of crab patterns to permit, which are especially spooky; or when tarpon are moving over white sand. (When tarpon are moving over a dark bottom, such as one covered in turtle grass, they aren't nearly as spooky as when they are cruising over white sand. Apparently, tarpon know that their dark green backs provide camouflage on a grass-covered bottom. But that same dark back makes them stand out like a black mark on white paper when they swim over a light colored bottom.)

While many fly fishermen generally use six to nine-foot leaders for tarpon, when these giants cruise over a light bottom, often a leader as long as 16 feet is called for in order to drop a fly so that it doesn't frighten the fish. Keep in mind that heavy 10 to 13-weight tarpon lines come down mighty hard. In conditions when the fish may be easily spooked, lengthening the leader is the answer.

When fishing for permit and tarpon, in conditions such as I have described above, it's a good idea to use a butt section of 40-pound test monofilament. Select a butt section in a length you prefer (about six feet is what I use), and for each succeeding piece of lighter mono, add one half the length of the previous length of monofilament. Then complete the leader by adding 24 inches of tippet. For example, if you start with a butt section of six feet of 40-pound test, then add three feet of 30-pound, then one and a half feet of 20-pound, then nine inches of 15-pound, and complete the rig with a final tippet of 24 inches of 12-pound, you'll have

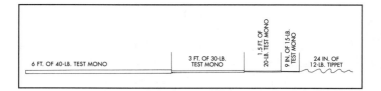

Typical Long Saltwater Tapered Leader

a tapered leader with total length of a little over 13 feet that turns over a tarpon or permit fly very well. I have also used this formula on bonefish, steelheads, bass and many other situations where a long tapered leader is called for.

But keep in mind that when you are building one of these tapered leaders, *you should not use stiff monofilament in the butt section,* despite the myth to the contrary that has been around for generations. The reason is this: when you stop the rod on your forward cast, the line unrolls to deposit the fly at the target site. If the soft unrolling fly line comes to the leader and the butt section is very stiff, the butt section resists unrolling and can impede the cast. A less rigid butt section will do better.

Keep in mind also that while this formula works well for constructing any long tapered leader, *it should not be used for dry-fly fishing.* For dry-fly fishing, special tapered leaders (which can be purchased at any fly shop) should be employed.

I could discuss many other examples of where a longer leader is essential for good presentations — especially to the particularly difficult fish. I guess the point I'm making is to not be stuck with a prescribed leader length for all your fishing. You should be willing to adjust leader length when you feel it will help.

As I will be pointing out several times in this book (and it's worth repeating), perhaps one of the most frequently violated principles of presentation technique that I see is that of an angler dropping his fly either on top of or too close to a fish.

Remember, the two major reasons for a leader are: to allow the fly to have more action (it wouldn't if it were tied to the fly line); and to keep the impact of the fly line hitting the water well away from the fish.

While it may not necessarily matter in making presentations to fish lying in very deep water, I can't think of any shallow water fly-fishing situation where your chances are enhanced if the fly line falls on top of or too close to a fish. You need to be very much aware that at all times your fly line should fall well away from any fish you hope to catch. That is why long leaders are so necessary on very calm water.

Presentations with Short Leaders

When using sinking lines in any waters that are not crystal clear and quiet, short leaders — *less than three feet long!* — should be used. Of course, on very clear waters, such as on many impoundment lakes, beaver ponds and similar waters, you will need a longer leader. But wherever there is flowing water or the water is the least bit cloudy, a short leader is an asset when fishing a sinking fly line.

Also, leaders shorter than normal need to be used when casting bulky or heavy flies. Standard tapered leaders don't have enough stiffness in the mid-portion to turn over such patterns, unless the angler has been able to deliver a very high speed cast.

TIPPET SELECTION

Another important factor in making a good presentation is that the angler needs to consider the tippet being used in relationship to the size of the fly being presented. The type of hook, its size, its weight, and how it is dressed, are important considerations.

Regarding tippets for dry flies, trout fishermen for years have been following a rule that prescribes that if you want to know what X size tippet to use, divide the size of the hook by three (some say four). For example, the rule says that if you are using a size 12 dry fly, divide by three, and use a 4X tippet. A similar rule that arrives at pretty much the same place is that you should multiply the tippet size by three to determine the correct hook size for any tippet. Thus, if you were using a 4X tippet, three times that would dictate the use of a size 12 hook.

Like a lot of general rules that have been around a long time, this one doesn't work. Because on the same size hook, a number of dry-fly patterns may be dressed entirely differently, and have entirely different casting and stream presentation characteristics.

Fly Dressing Effects Tippet Selection

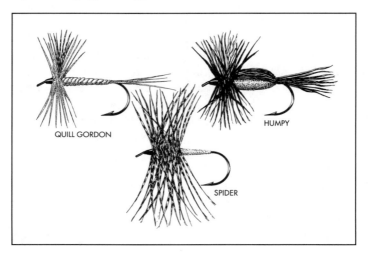

QUILL GORDON

HUMPY

SPIDER

For example, take a Quill Gordon, a Humpy and a spider, all of them tied on hooks of the same conformation, weight and size. The Quill Gordon is a Catskill-type tie, in which very little material is used and the fly is dressed quite sparsely. The Humpy, on the other hand, uses lots of material, and if anything, a good Humpy would be considered to be an overdressed dry fly. A spider is dressed with hackles that are several sizes larger than what is normally called for, so that it has a hackle diameter at least twice that of either the Quill Gordon or the Humpy.

Any experienced fly caster examining these three patterns would instantly realize that these three flies have grossly different air resistance characteristics in flight and therefore cast very differently.

So forget those simple formulas that tell you what tippet size should be matched to a particular hook size. The only way you can be sure that your tippet will be matched to your fly is for you to tie on a dry fly, cast it and observe how it falls to the surface.

A correct presentation is one in which the tippet falls in soft waves (or a series of small "S" curves), between the fly and the next larger portion of the tapered leader. With this type of presentation, the current pushing against the tippet cannot create drag on the fly until it has first eliminated the "S" curves. Thus a drag-free drift of the fly results.

But if the tippet collapses so that part falls forward of the fly and part falls to the side or rear in a curved shape resembling a horseshoe, you'll probably accomplish a drag-free drift, but you will not have made an accurate cast. Presentations of this type occur when the tippet section is either too long or thin, and not enough casting energy is being transmitted through the leader to turn the fly over.

On the other hand, if the tippet falls so that it describes a straight line between the fly and the next larger portion of

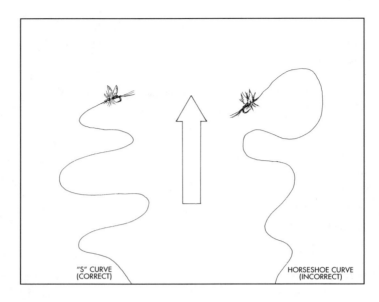

"S" CURVE
(CORRECT)

HORSESHOE CURVE
(INCORRECT)

Dry-Fly Tippet Presentation

the leader — with no waves in it — you have a tippet that is either too short or too thick, and it is transmitting so much casting energy through the leader that everything straightens. The current will immediately push against such a straight tippet, which in turn will create drag on the fly.

What the dry-fly fisherman is trying to do is make a cast in which the tippet *almost* straightens. This serves to provide accuracy on the cast, while at the same time creates soft waves, or "S" curves, between the fly and the next heavier portion of the leader.

Because everyone casts slightly differently, you cannot generalize as to the correct leader and tippet rig that will create this type presentation in identical fashion for everyone. To get a leader so that the tippet falls with soft, desirable waves immediately in back of the fly, each angler needs to make personal adjustments to the leader and tippet for himself. What works for one person may not work perfectly for another.

The better the caster you are, the more you can adjust the cast to accommodate the leader. If you want to make a drag-free presentation to a fish, you need to tie the fly on the tippet and make a few casts. If the tippet falls back on itself, either shorten the tippet or replace it with one that is heavier and stiffer. If it falls straight out in front of the fly, you need to either lengthen the existing tippet, or replace it with one that is longer or less rigid.

With underwater flies, the angler's objective should be to present the fly so that it moves through the water column in a natural manner. If it doesn't, the fish will be alerted and strikes are not likely to be forthcoming.

Suppose you are fishing small nymphs, for example, size 14 to 20, in slow-moving water. The fish is holding in the water column, taking in drifting nymphs as they wobble and drift freely with the current. If you attach a heavy tippet (heavy being 2X or larger for a size 14 to 22 nymph), you will kill the fly's action in the current. Tying such a large, stiff monofilament tippet to a tiny fly is like welding an unyielding iron rod to the hook. The fly will not be able to sweep freely in the currents in the pool, and will look very unrealistic as it approaches any wise trout.

I've seen this same thing happen when an angler has lost two or three large bonefish on light tippets in the six to 10-pound test range. Frustrated by these break-offs, the angler then decides to go to a much heavier tippet, and attaches a small size 4 or 6 bonefish fly to 15-pound test tippet. This tippet is so large and stiff in relation to the small fly that it kills all the fly's action.

If existing fishing conditions force you to use a tippet that by examination is ruining the action of the fly on the

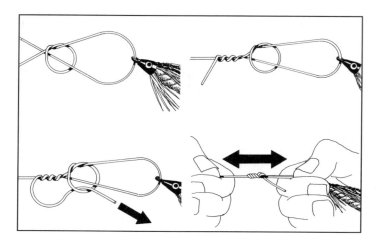

Non-Slip Mono-loop Knot

retrieve, then rather than increase tippet weight, you should instead employ an alternative technique: make a loop knot that will allow the fly to swing freely. The Uni-knot (first called the Duncan Loop) will do, but my favorite is the non-slip Mono-loop, the strongest of the loop knots.

Now let's look at shock tippets. The shock tippet needs to be considered for making presentations in saltwater to such sharp-toothed fish as barracuda or bluefish; or for freshwater presentations to powerful run-to-construction species such as the South American peacock bass or the Australian Spaniard mackerel.

A shock tippet is simply a length of wire or heavy monofilament — generally cut to a relatively short length — attached between the regular tippet and the fly. You may find it difficult to believe, but the long shock tippets that are advocated by many fly fishermen (and even some guides) can spoil your presentation, as they offer considerably more resistance to turning the fly over than you might imagine, unless you have tried it. And in clear water a long shock tippet may alarm the fish and buy you only a refusal.

For these reasons, when using wire for my shock tippet, I rarely use a piece longer than the width of my hand. And when using monofilament for shock tippets, I use 60 to 120-pound test (the size being determined by the species I am after) in a length no longer than 10 or 11 inches.

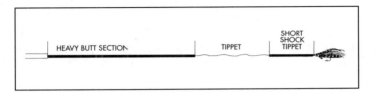

Typical Shock Tippet Leader Rig

FLY SELECTION

In making your presentation, the type of fly that you throw may require an adjustment in your casting. There is a great deal of difference between what could be called a bulky fly and one that is heavy.

Bulky flies — such as large Dahlberg Divers, popping bugs and deer hair bugs — tend to slow the line down, and in the wind are a bit difficult to cast. But you can still employ a conventional casting motion with this type fly, maybe adding a little faster rod tip acceleration and a bit quicker pumping action on the double haul to aid in turning the bulky fly over, especially if there is a slight breeze.

But when you are using heavy flies — large epoxy flies such as a surf candy or permit crab patterns, large Clouser deep minnows loaded with 1/8 or 1/10-ounce lead eyes, or whistler fly patterns (which have either lead eyes or bead chain eyes to make them sink faster) — or when you are using split-shot, which similarly adds unusual weight to the tippet, your casting stroke has to be altered if you want to make a good presentation.

Here's an instance where you *don't want to cast a tight loop!* A tight loop will often cause the leader to tangle. And if a good cast is made with a tight loop, almost too much speed is generated and the fly slams over and into the water, almost always spooking any nearby fish.

With heavy flies, a wider, more open loop is recommended. It's also a good idea when making presentations with heavier flies (not necessarily with bulky flies) that the cast be tilted to the side slightly, so that you don't get hit with that heavy fly on the back or forward cast.

Heavy Fly Casting: Incorrect and Correct Technique

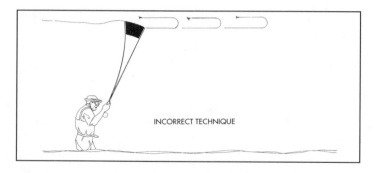

INCORRECT TECHNIQUE

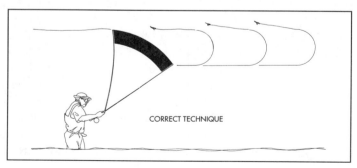

CORRECT TECHNIQUE

Using flies (and fly lines) for purposes other than that for which they were originally designed can also be a deadly technique in some circumstances.

For example, modifying a sinking-tip line and fishing it with a floating bass bug or Dahlberg Diver is a great method of fishing for bass, snook and baby tarpon. To do this, modify a standard sinking-tip line by cutting off five feet of its 10-foot sink tip, leaving five feet of sinking tip on the remaining line. Attach a leader from six to seven feet long, and tie on a popping bug or Dahlberg Diver. This modified sinking-tip line rig now gives you an effective instrument for an especially deadly retrieving technique.

Here's how to use it. Make a cast into a spot where you feel a bass, baby tarpon or snook may be. If you start retrieving as soon as the popper hits the surface, and continue to retrieve, the popper will stay on the surface and pop in the same manner as if you were using a full floating line. But, make a few strips on the line, causing the popper to pop and gurgle, and then stop retrieving. If your pause is long enough, the short sinking section of the line will drag the popper beneath the surface. Once it disappears, start stripping line again. As you do, you will loft the sinking portion of the line to the surface, bringing the popper up with it. Then as you continue to strip, the popper will again pop and gurgle. Now, stop retrieving. The popper will sink below the surface again. Using this technique you can fish the popper on the surface for as long as you like, then swim it underwater for brief periods, and then repeat the operation. It's a devastating technique for those times when conventional retrieves are failing to produce strikes.

Another way to accomplish this retrieve is through the use of a full-sinking line and a *long* leader — at least 12 feet in length — and a popping bug. Using this rig will give you a similar but slightly different retrieving effect.

Here's how to use this rig. Make a long cast. Give the fly line time to sink to the bottom, or at least a considerable distance down into the water column. The popper will be dragged well below the surface. Then begin your retrieve. As the stripping continues, the line will straighten and this will cause the popper to dive even deeper into the water. Stop your retrieve. The line will start sinking, but the popper will begin to swim towards the surface. Repeat this retrieve-and-stop method. This will cause the popper to swim forward and up, then down, then up, etc. throughout the retrieve.

One situation where this technique is highly effective is when you want to draw fish out from underneath a boat dock. Cast parallel to the dock and allow the popper to sink deep, retrieving the fly alongside the pilings in an up-and-down motion. I do not know of any other fly-fishing rig that accomplishes this purpose so effectively.

BASIC RULES FOR SELECTING LINES, LEADERS, TIPPETS AND FLIES

1. Under calm conditions, use the lightest floating line possible and you will up your score considerably on most species in both fresh and saltwater.
2. In evaluating a sinking line, the important consideration is how *well* it sinks to the depth in the water column that the angler perceives the fish to be in, and therefore where he wants to position his fly. For this reason, for most fishing situations, the sinking-tip line and conventional full-sinking fly lines are not good presentation instruments. Uniform-sinking lines, Teeny Nymph lines, and various types of sinking shooting heads are better.
3. The correct length of a shooting head is the length you can hold outside the rod tip and false cast comfortably.

4. In trout fishing, the more wary the fish, and the calmer the water, the longer the leader needed.

5. When using sinking lines in any waters that are not crystal clear and quiet, short leaders — less than three feet long — should be used.

6. When you are using heavy (as opposed to bulky) flies, or tippets weighted with split-shot, you must alter your casting stroke. Do not cast a tight loop. A wider, more open loop is recommended.

OVERLEAF: *Poul Jorgensen at Blue Sea Falls on the Cane River, North Carolina.*

CHAPTER FOUR

PRESENTATION AND RETRIEVING TACTICS

I would like to suggest for your consideration some basic presentation and retrieving tactics that apply to almost all fly-fishing situations in either fresh or saltwater environments — whether you are fishing for tarpon or brook trout, whether you are on a quiet beaver pond, a small mountain stream, or a mile-wide saltwater flat.

GET AS CLOSE AS YOU CAN

Unless you are an exceptional fly caster, the closer you can get to a fish (within reason — you don't want the fish to see you), the better your chances. Accuracy comes from being close and not pushing yourself to the limits of your casting abilities.

THE FIRST CAST IS THE MOST IMPORTANT

The first cast is the most important one, so make it as perfect as you possibly can. All too often we rush as we make the first cast. A trout fisherman will see a trout sipping dry flies. He quickly gets into position, hastily strips off line and makes a cast. Because of the rush, the cast is flawed and the trout is alerted. Now, things become increasingly more difficult, and each successive cast reduces the chances for a hook-up.

In saltwater the time factor is decreased. The reason for this is that while in trout fishing the water is moving and the fish is not, in saltwater the water is relatively still and the fish is moving. We have only the time that the cruising fish is within casting distance to make a presentation. The rapid movement of the fish (along with urgent messages from the guide) generally puts most anglers under severe pressure. Of all areas of fly fishing, I think more rushed casts are made in shallow saltwater flats fishing than in all other situations.

Remember, that first cast is vital. The time difference between rushing the cast and slowing down enough to gain control of what you are doing, may only be two or three seconds — but that interval can make the difference between a good presentation and a poor one.

UNDERWATER FLIES NEED TO BE PRESENTED NATURALLY

While very early in the game anglers learn that dry flies need to be presented to trout with a natural-appearing drag-free drift, perhaps one of the most important and least understood techniques of presenting underwater flies is how they approach the fish.

Since it was big enough to eat minnows, a brown trout has seen all minnows flee when it gets too near. Crayfish seek shelter and try to hide from smallmouth bass. A crab on a saltwater flat will dive for the bottom and attempt to hide once it sees a predator, such as a permit. Shrimp flee at the slightest hint of a bonefish. And on the open ocean, a flying fish takes flight the moment a large predator enters the area.

No minnow ever picks a fight with a predatory fish. Nor does a crayfish attack a smallmouth bass. A crab doesn't assault a permit, and certainly no baitfish in the open sea will attack a billfish. *Yet, many fly fishermen present and retrieve their underwater flies in an aggressive posture to predator fish all the time. It is one of the major reasons why predatory fish refuse such presentations*

Before explaining the technique for presenting and retrieving an underwater fly in a natural manner, let's look at the fish's viewpoint of the food it eats. A bonefish cruising across a flat sees a shrimp or crab in the water near it. If the food is up-current from the bonefish, the tide will usually be sweeping the prey toward the bonefish. As the prey sees the bonefish, it tries to dart off to the side and escape.

Or when a trout, salmon, steelhead or bass is holding in the current, food is being brought to it from upstream. It sees a minnow, crayfish or sculpin being swept toward it in the flow. If the prey sees the fish in time, it will also dart off to one side, or dive for the bottom.

No prey species is going to swim against the current close to the predator fish. Nor is any prey species going to come across the current directly at or from behind a predator. This would be unnatural behavior. *Yet, this is exactly how many anglers present and retrieve their underwater flies.*

Any fly that imitates underwater food (excepting nymphs, which, like dry flies, should be presented to the fish drag-free) should approach the fish naturally. Where there is a freshwater current or tidal flow, the force of the water will naturally transport food morsels to fish. Thus, a fly fished from upstream and on the flow toward the fish has a more natural appearance than any fly that is cast downstream of the fish and brought back against the current. If there is any unnatural motion to the fly, the fish will either hesitate or flee.

Now here are some examples of how anglers present underwater flies improperly, and how to correct that presentation fault.

A trout fisherman is walking along the shoreline, or wading carefully along the edge. Suddenly, a fish is seen lying out in the current, slightly upstream of the angler. The angler crouches, makes a cast and the fly drops slightly upstream and to the far side of the fish. A retrieve is started and the fly moves down and back across the stream toward the fish. The trout sees the fly coming and it moves forward to investigate. The fly keeps coming directly toward the trout. As it gets very near, the fly continues to swim even closer to the trout. The fish hesitates (this is something it has never seen before, a prey species actually appears to be attacking it!), and then bolts.

A similar situation occurs when fishing for bonefish, or any other fish cruising on a saltwater flat. The angler is being poled against the tide across the flats by the guide. A bonefish is seen off to the side and slightly in front of the boat swimming into the tide. The angler casts well up-current from the fish and slightly to the far side of it. The retrieve is again started, and as line is recovered, the fly swims directly at the bonefish. The bonefish has never seen its food swim directly at it, so it figures something has to be wrong and flees.

How do you make an underwater presentation in these two typically encountered situations?

In the first (trout) example, the angler should move upstream of the fish. If he makes the cast from a position downstream of the fish, the fly will have to be brought back in such a manner as to appear to attack the fish. If there is no chance of doing this, the fly can be cast directly ahead and to the side of the fish and the retrieve started. This will bring the fly back on the angler's side of the predator so that it does not appear to be attacking the fish.

But the ideal situation would be to get upstream of the fish. A cast is now made that allows the angler to cast well ahead and on the far side of the fish. The target area should be such that the fly can be retrieved properly. Properly retrieved means that the fly is brought back and as it arrives just in front of the fish, it makes a turn and comes back towards the angler. In these circumstances, what the fish sees is apparently a species approaching on the current, then suddenly turning to the side and fleeing. This is a natural occurrence that has happened many times, so the predator streaks forward and grabs the offering.

In the second (bonefish) example, where the angler sees a cruising fish, an attempt should be made to get into a position well ahead of the fish — just as the angler did on the stationary trout. Then a cast is made to the far side and ahead of the fish. The fly should be retrieved so that it is brought back and just in front of the fish, and then makes a sweeping turn away from the fish. Again, so far as the

Fly Swimming at Fish — Incorrect Presentation

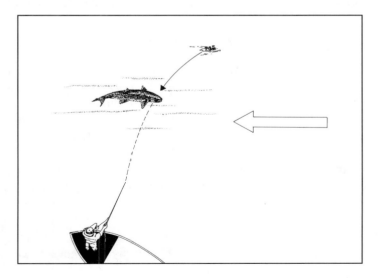

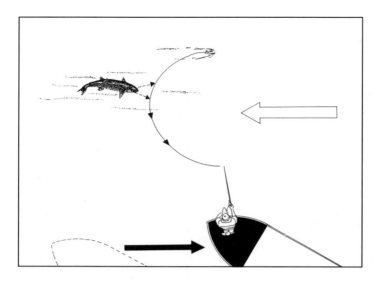

Fly Swimming in Front of Fish — Correct Presentation

bonefish can tell, this is a natural prey and it will usually take the fly.

Another situation presents itself when the angler is up-current (or up-tide) from the fish and the fish is facing in the direction of the angler. Most anglers will throw the fly directly in front of the predator. But that is not the best way to make the presentation. If the fish is very close — less than 25 feet away — on your retrieve you will draw the fish close to you as it follows your offering, radically increasing the odds that the fish will see you and spook.

Instead, make a curve cast that causes the fly to land well off to one side of the fish, with the leader lying at right angles to the fish. (It's important that the end of the fly line not fall on the fish!) Now as you begin your retrieve, the fly will follow the path of the leader and curve you have put in the line, which, in turn, will cause the fly to swim across and in front of the fish, from one side to the other. The fish will thus be able to observe the fly swimming through the water column for more than 10 feet before the fly turns and starts tracking toward the angler. Thus the fish has considerable time to observe and chase the fly with a reduced chance of seeing the angler.

The curve cast is a very easy one to make. If the fish is directly in front of you, make a *side cast*. The rod should travel parallel to the water for this cast — never in a slightly downward motion. As the rod sweeps forward and there is about a 45-degree angle between both the angler and the fish, make a very sudden, sharp acceleration, coupled with a dead stop.

If you know how to double haul, making a strong, short haul at the same time will help. You want to make this cast as hard as you can. This is one of the few times when you really want to apply power during the very brief last portion of the cast. What you want to do is cause the rod tip to accelerate very rapidly, and stop dead! This causes the tip to

Curve Cast: Fish in Front of Angler

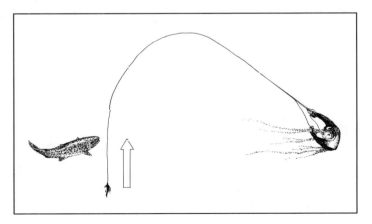

sweep forward in a deep curve. That curve is transmitted to the line and a large curve results at the line and leader end.

If you have made your rod stop at an angle of 45 degrees between you and the fish, you can throw a very accurate curve. But be careful not to throw the line close to the fish. You want only the leader to travel in front of the fish.

Another situation in which many anglers reduce their chances of catching a fish is when they are casting to the bank of a stream. The procedure followed by a lot of fly fishermen is to throw the fly at a spot slightly upstream and across the current, with the fly landing close to the bank. For the first foot or two the fly swims along the bank. Then, the current pushing against the fly line forces the fly to swim *away* from the bank. From this point until another cast is made, the fish that are hiding along the bank can only see the narrow profile of the rear of the fly.

A much more effective cast is to make the curve cast (just as I explained above). In this case, the cast is made

Curve Cast: Fish Close to Bank

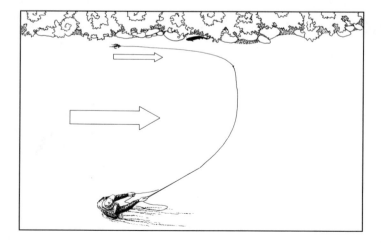

along the bank, with the front portion of the fly line and leader falling *parallel* to the back. Now the fly will swim for an extended period of time *along the shoreline*. This gives the fish a view of the much larger side profile of the fly pattern as it passes by, just as it perceives its natural food that is being swept by the current along the bank. Why else do you think the fish would be holding there?

In yet another tactical situation, if the fish is lying directly down current, farther than 20 or 25 feet away and facing you, don't throw the fly directly in front of the fish. Instead, throw the fly three to four feet off to the side and about even with the fish's head. As you retrieve, the fish will see the fly's motion as it looks off to the side. And what it will see — or thinks it's seeing — is what appears to be a prey attempting to escape. From the fish's viewpoint, this retrieve looks far more realistic and less threatening than one where the offering drops on its nose and begins moving slowly away.

Fly Swimming Away from Fish — Correct Presentation

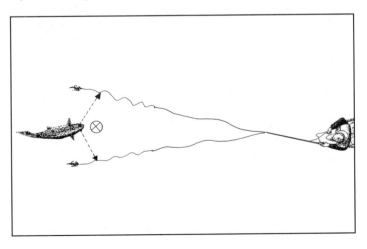

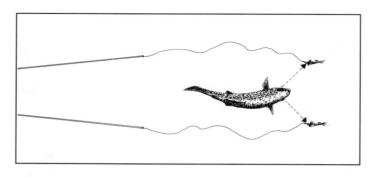

Angler Behind Fish — Correct Presentation

Now take an exactly opposite situation, when the fish is directly in front of you, facing away from you First keep in mind one of my cardinal rules of fly fishing never throw the fly line over the fish. And, when possible, don't drop the leader on the surface above a fish, either. Because if you throw the fly directly ahead of the fish, even though the leader may not spook it, you are still in trouble as your retrieve will bring the fly swimming directly at the fish, an unnatural occurrence. The fish will almost always flee.

What is required is to throw the fly several feet forward and to one side of the fish. Begin your retrieve. The fish sees something moving off to the side. Its prey appears to be sneaking away and the fish will pursue it.

There is yet another effective retrieving technique that can be used when the angler is fishing an underwater fly toward a bank that is relatively clear of brush and trees. This happens a great deal of the time in saltwater, where oyster bars or mud or sandy banks exist. Lakes that are subject to a draw-down (leaving bare banks) are also candidates for this technique.

For this special retrieve you need a long leader, at least 12 feet in length. And, you will want a fast-sinking line. The

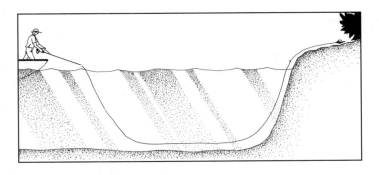

Fishing Clear Bank: the Cast

selection of the fly is important, too. You will need either a bend-back style fly (a specialty fly available in many fly shops) or a fly equipped with a weedguard.

Holding well off the bank, make a long cast so that *the fly, leader, and some of the fly line land on the dry bank.* Don't start your retrieve immediately. Instead, allow the line that

Fishing Clear Bank: the Retrieve

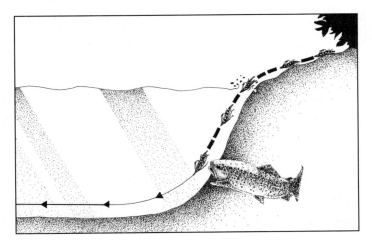

fell to the water to sink to the bottom of the water. Now begin a slow retrieve. If you make the retrieve slowly, the sinking line will not loft up off the bottom and the fly will crawl across the dry bank and enter the water. Continue a slow retrieve and the sinking line that has remained on the bottom will cause the fly to be dragged down along the side of the bank wall, down to the bottom, and then across. A fish holding along the bank's wall will see this morsel crawling down from above and will usually strike.

When fishing a stream in deep water (five to 10-foot depths, for example), there is another trick that often produces well in both fresh and saltwater. You'll need a fast-sinking fly line for this, with a leader no more than three feet long. Again, you should use a bend-back style streamer fly, or one equipped with a weedguard. But for this technique, the most important factor is that your fly have a spe-

Special Deep Water Fly Presentation

cial wing made from a buoyant material (I favor bucktail), and be dressed with more material than normal. What you want is a wing that is really buoyant. (Such a buoyant wing pattern is a specialty item you will not likely find in a fly shop; you will have to tie it yourself or commission one from a professional fly tyer.)

The fly is cast out and the line allowed to sink until it contacts the bottom. Now the retrieve starts. Don't rush it, just move the fly along slowly. Since a slow retrieve will allow the fast-sinking line to stay in contact with the bottom, and because the fly is buoyant, the streamer will ride just a few inches above the bottom.

This is a deadly technique when fishing for snook or redfish that are holding in a channel, or when fishing for bass when they are taking crayfish off the river or lake floor.

LEARN HOW FLIES AND BAITFISH MOVE IN WATER

We have discussed how it is important for the angler to understand that the angle at which his imitation is presented and retrieved towards the fish is one of the keys to the fish perceiving it as natural food. But there are some additional factors other than the angle or direction at which the fly comes to the fish that create the impression of a natural approach. Knowledge of how flies and baitfish move along or through the water column can also significantly improve your retrieving technique.

For example, take dry-fly fishing. Most of the time when a trout is taking dry flies, the fish is holding in a specific position in the current. It waits for insects to drift to it. It doesn't move throughout the pool, but holds in a very specific location. Because it is lying in one place, it is very much aware of the specific currents that are bringing the insect to it. *It is important to understand that the trout only has to know how flies are drifting toward it in the particular current under which it is holding, not how all the currents are coursing throughout the entire pool.*

If every fly that the trout has been capturing has come to it with a natural drift which is, say, moving slightly to the left and then sweeping back to the right as it passes over the fish, then the fish will probably refuse a fly drifting to it from any other direction or in any other manner.

If you are able to determine the trout's feeding behavior in this regard as it makes rise after rise, you should obviously try to imitate a similar drift with your fly. *And it's very important that in doing this that you allow your fly to drift drag-free from the time the fish first sees it until the take.* And remember, making a cast so that the tippet falls to the water with soft waves in the first foot or so closest to the fly is vital to achieving that drag-free drift.

Almost as soon as people begin dry-fly fishing, they become aware that drag is a problem, even if they don't know how to correct it. But when they take up nymphing, most trout fishermen are not aware that achieving a drag-free drift can be even more important than when dry-fly fishing.

Except for very large trout (which normally don't feed on small flies, but prefer to eat larger morsels, such as other fish, crayfish or sculpins), the major food supply for most of the trout in the stream are underwater insects. That means that they get a large part of their food from drifting emergers or nymphs. So trout are actually much more aware of the improper or unnatural drifting of a nymph that is coming towards them in the water column than they are of an unnaturally drifting dry fly moving across the surface. Yet many nymph fishermen virtually ignore this fact.

For a drag-free drift, *when presenting a nymph, try to fish with as short a line as possible.* The longer the line, the more chance the current has to ruin the natural drift of your offering. Achieving a drag-free drift is one of the generally unrecognized advantages of nymph fishing with a strike indicator. The strike indicator works to suspend the nymph in the water column, creating a more realistic drift to the fly.

In presenting and retrieving either dry flies or nymphs, there are times, however, when more specialized techniques of manipulating the fly — by twitching the line, raising the rod, or giving some other unusual action — will definitely draw more strikes from a reluctant fish. I will be discussing these specialized techniques in considerable detail in my upcoming book on trout fishing in the Library, *Fly Fishing for Trout (Volume I)*.

From the viewpoint of understanding not only the trout's behavior, but also that of its prey, many anglers also fish sculpin patterns improperly. The sculpin, a small catfish-like minnow that lives on the bottom of many freshwater streams, is a major source of protein, and is eagerly sought after by bass, trout, and other freshwater species.

What do we need to know about a sculpin to make a proper imitative retrieve?

First, that sculpins are primarily nocturnal organisms — at least they certainly move around more at night or at dawn or dusk. Consequently fishing sculpin patterns in the middle of the day will likely not bring you a strike, unless a fish is *very* hungry. So fish them early or late in the day, or after dark.

Next, sculpins have no swim bladder, so the moment they stop swimming they sink toward the bottom. For this reason you will almost always find sculpins close to or smack on the bottom. What this means is that we should present a sculpin imitation that sinks quickly to the bottom, and because it will be moving across the bottom, it should be equipped with either a monofilament or wire weedguard, or be tied reverse style (with the hook pointed up), so that the angler can retrieve it effectively through bottom grasses. (Working a sculpin high in the water column may occasionally catch you a fish, but most of the time it is a futile exercise.)

And since the sculpin depends upon camouflage to escape detection from predators, it will almost always be the color of the bottom over which it swims. Generally speaking, an olive or tarnish-colored sculpin is the color to imitate.

A saltwater example of where an understanding of prey behavior becomes important to retrieving technique is to consider a crab that feels threatened by a permit. As soon as the crab realizes a permit is nearby, it dives for the bottom. It tilts its flat body to an angle of descent of about 45 degrees and travels as fast as it can to the bottom. Once there it holds its claws aloft and lies motionless, for it doesn't want to draw attention to itself. It can't swim fast, so it depends upon its camouflaged coloration and immobility to prevent discovery.

How does this information help the permit fisherman plan his retrieve?

First, properly selecting the correct imitation is helpful. Many crab patterns float, and since that is not usually the best profile for enticing a permit to strike, are weighted with a heavy material or coating on their underside to make the fly sink. But more often than not, a crab pattern coated in this manner settles to the bottom somewhat like a saucer that is placed flat on the surface of a pan of water, undulating back and forth as it slowly sinks.

A better pattern design is one that looks somewhat like a crab sinking quickly as it tilts its body to one side and dives for the bottom. This is usually achieved by positioning lead eyes on one edge of the imitation crab. One favorite pattern of this type is Del's Merkin, which imitates the crab's descent very well.

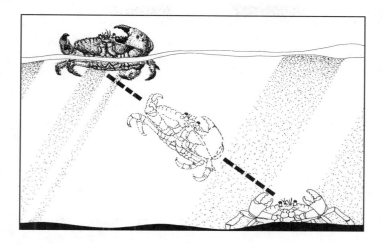

Typical Descent of Crab

When presenting and retrieving such patterns to a permit, the angler should not continuously move the fly along the bottom. That is not what a crab would do when threatened by the permit. Instead, when the angler sees the permit, a cast should be made so that the fly is thrown far enough ahead not to spook the fish, but still draw its atten-

Typical Crab Patterns

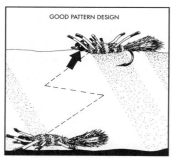

tion to the offering. As a general rule, this would be from eight to 10 feet in front of the permit. The fly is then retrieved *along the surface* until the permit sees it. At this time, the angler allows the fly to drop as quickly as possible to the bottom. After the fly settles on the bottom, even though you may be tempted to, don't move it. Tighten the line so you can feel when and if the permit picks up the fly.

Sometimes the permit will circle the fly. This species has particularly keen eyesight, so don't worry too much about it not seeing your offering. But if the permit seems to lose interest and begins to move away, only then should you make a few twitches to barely move the fly.

If anglers do anything wrong when offering crab patterns to permit, they tend to over-manipulate the crab, showing the permit something that appears unnatural.

These sculpin and crab examples are offered to demonstrate that consciously attempting to imitate how the prey species act and the predator in turn reacts is an important retrieving technique.

LEARN THE ANATOMY AND FEEDING BEHAVIOR OF FISH

A fish's anatomy and feeding behavior substantially dictate where in the water column you should offer the fly.

Although they will occasionally rise to take an offering, species such as bonefish and redfish, which are primarily bottom feeders, have eyes and mouth located on the lower portion of the skull so that they see and feed in a downward direction. For such fish, offering your fly near or on the bottom will increase your chances of a hook-up.

But species that have their eyes and mouths located higher up on the skull, so that they see and feed either straight ahead or up, such as tarpon, will almost never descend to take a fly.

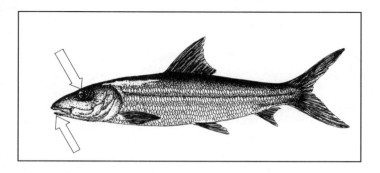

Typical Bottom-Feeding Fish Anatomy

Feeding behavior also dictates fly selection. While a trout will feed at a number of depths, when it is on station in a deep pool, feeding exclusively on nymphs tight against the bottom, it will rarely rise to take a nymph that is floating along just under the surface.

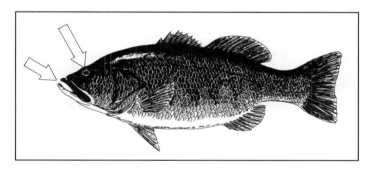

Typical Top-Feeding Fish Anatomy

Having a knowledge of the fish you pursue, and at what depth in the water column they are feeding, are decided assets in presentation and retrieving tactics. Once this factor is understood, the proper fly line selection (Do you want the fly near the top of the water or to descend well below?), and the sink rate of the fly become very important factors in successful fly fishing in either fresh or saltwater.

PAY ATTENTION TO BOTTOM COLORATION

Whenever you are seeking bottom-feeding species of fish, or you are fishing with flies that imitate prey species that live on the bottom, if you are not sure what to use, always start with a fly that closely matches the bottom coloration. A prey species bearing a color that contrasted markedly with the bottom would never have evolved, since it would have been seen and quickly captured by predatory fish long ago. Over the the ages, such species would have either changed their basic coloration, or they wouldn't have survived.

Two examples come to mind, one in fresh-water and one in saltwater, to prove this point.

In Alaska, most of the sculpins (a major food source for rainbow trout after the salmon eggs are gone) are brownish/olive, the color of most stream bed gravel. My experience when fishing sculpins in Alaska is that an olive sculpin fly will out-fish any other color, three to one.

And when fishing on the light sand flats of the Bahamas, Los Roques, Christmas Island, and similar areas, flies that are light in color will consistently catch more bonefish.

There is an exception to this, however. In many inshore saltwater areas where I have fished, if the water has been roiled by heavy tidal flows, silt can remain suspended in the water and be constantly kept in motion by tidal rises and falls for a very long time, forcing the fish to feed in muddy water, or at best, water that is rarely clear. In such situations, dark colored flies (black, purple, brown, or a combination of these colors) will usually out-fish other patterns, regardless of the bottom coloration.

CHANGE YOUR RETRIEVING METHOD TO PRODUCE RESULTS

Fishermen are like everyone else, I suppose. We get into habits that we tend to follow unthinkingly all the time. But remember this: *one of the most important rules of retrieving is to change your retrieving technique if your present method is not producing results.* This is especially true if you can see a fish following your fly and it refuses to take. Do something different! Frequently this means imitating the behavior of a crippled fish.

Observing predator fish in the open sea is instructive in this regard. When they discover a school of baitfish, they don't just dash in and try to gobble the bait. Instead, they look for any small fish that may seem to be ailing or weak. If any baitfish appears to be crippled or unable to swim at top speed, the predators streak in and grab it.

So when fish are consistently refusing your underwater offerings, you may be able to tempt a big bass, barracuda, snook, redfish, or numerous other fresh and saltwater species by switching to a streamer or a popping bug. These patterns will help you give the impression to the fish that your offering is a crippled creature, resulting in a higher percentage of strikes.

In many of these situations, the popper is preferred, because you can easily manipulate a popper to make it appear to be struggling on the surface, as if it were a fish injured or in trouble; while a streamer swimming below the surface — no matter how large it is — must appear to the fish as if it were in good shape and would offer a hard chase if pursued.

Another advantage of popping bugs is that you can create an illusion that the prey you are attempting to imitate is really much bigger than it actually is, whereas a streamer or other underwater pattern worked in front of a fish can be clearly seen by the fish so that it can determine how big it is, which may not be large enough for its appetite!

Where this tip really proves its worth for me is whenever I am fly fishing for two saltwater species in particular: amberjack and cobia. I have never been able to tie a fly large enough to tempt amberjack or cobia in excess of 50 pounds to take my fly, unless the fish was properly teased beforehand. So after casting even 12-inch long streamers to amberjack and cobia with no luck, I've switched to a big popping bug (maybe only half or two-thirds as long as the streamer pattern) and achieved a strike. I believe that the loud splashing and continuous noise of the popper makes the amberjack or cobia think that here is something really worth taking!

There are wide ranges of opinions about how to retrieve a popping bug. The correct procedure is never set in stone, for sometimes a very slow retrieve, combined with a speed-up of the bug now and then, is best.

What usually governs how fast a popper should be retrieved involves the species sought, what the fish is doing at the time (Is it chasing bait or lying in wait?), and the watery environment of the fish. Largemouth bass in a Texas tank, where temperatures may be in the mid-80s, will not respond to a popping bug like a smallmouth lying behind a rock in a cool Minnesota lake. What is important to realize is that when using a popping bug, you will have to modify your retrieve for existing species and fishing conditions.

Changing your retrieving method is also recommended when you are getting numerous refusals from bonefish. Normally in bonefishing, a series of short strips, with the fly falling over and over again to the bottom, is most effective. But when that's not working, what can change a lazy bonefish into an aggressive predator that will tear into your fly is often a few long, fast pulls of the line. With this type retrieval, apparently the bonefish thinks the fly is escaping and when it sees it swimming swiftly, it moves in and attacks.

And on all species, there are some occasions when a fly that is normally retrieved with a good deal of action should be simply left in a dead-drifting position underneath or on the water, with no manipulation by the angler.

LEARN GOOD ROD-HANDLING TECHNIQUE

One factor to consider in retrieving technique is the angle of the rod during the time the fly approaches and passes near the fish. For many years a number of outdoor writers have implored bass fishermen not to manipulate their underwater flies and popping bugs with the rod tip, as this creates unwanted slack line when the rod tip is flipped upward and then dropped. This faulty rod technique is a major reason why many anglers miss strikes.

Rod angle during retrieve is important in fly fishing for almost all fish species. A good technique when nymph or dry-fly fishing for trout in fast water, after the offering is thrown upstream, is to strip the line and remove unwanted slack by raising the rod tip.

To prevent slack from developing when fishing streamers or other underwater flies, keep the tip in, or almost in, the water. And placing the rod tip underwater keeps the line straight between angler and fly, so that the angler can so much better feel the fish take the fly.

Mending the line (rolling the rod in an upstream or downstream arc to create a bow in the line), a technique learned by most anglers at an early stage in the development of their fly-fishing skills, is used routinely. But a closely related technique, following the fly with the rod tip during the drift to prevent a deep sag occurring in the mid-section of the fly line, while employed less frequently than line mending, is also a very important rod-handling technique for successful hook-ups.

In almost every kind of fly fishing, the angle at which the rod is held throughout the drift or retrieve makes a difference between hooking fish and not getting a strike.

LEARN GOOD LINE-HANDLING TECHNIQUE

Line technique — one of the most frequently overlooked elements of technique — is an important factor in presenting and retrieving the fly. In saltwater fly fishing, where you are sight fishing to bonefish, tarpon, redfish, etc., I believe good line control and technique can make all the difference between fishing success and failure.

If you use a spinning or plug rod, you would not think of simply throwing the lure in the direction of the target and not attempting to control its progress by using the first finger to trap the spinning line, or the thumb for trapping line from a casting reel. Yet, many fly fishermen simply turn the fly line loose on the cast.

Usually, when an angler makes a long cast (this also applies to many short casts, too) the rod is swept forward, stopped and the line released for the shoot. By saying released, I mean that the line is allowed to fall free of the hand. This can achieve a slightly longer distance on the cast. But it robs the angler of two vital presentation factors.

First, if the line is turned free and the fly streaks towards the target, after the rod stops you have no control whatsoever over how far the fly will travel. And second, once the fly line touches down, you must regain control of the fly line before you can manipulate the fly. These are serious technique flaws.

For accurate presentation of a fly, *never* turn the line loose at the end of the forward cast. Instead, make a giant "O" ring by cupping the fingers and allowing the thumb to stay in contact with the first two fingers. This gives you a large guide for the line to shoot through, but reduces your casting distance really very little.

In this position, as you watch the line unrolling, you can then close your fingers, trap the forward progress of the line, and drop your fly on the target whenever you choose.

Incidentally, a long-billed cap can impede your ability to see the line as it unrolls. And wearing no hat at all is nearly as bad. I much prefer a Florida Keys guide style hat for fish-

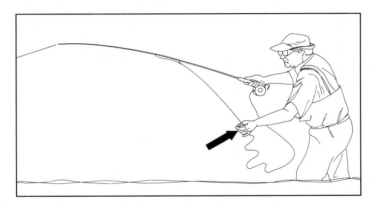

"O" Ring

ing. Its brim (about the same as any baseball cap) is ideal for being able to eliminate glare and still allows you to watch the unrolling fly line. And as I've discussed earlier in the book, I also think that in perhaps 90 percent of all fly-fishing situations, the use of a brightly colored line that is easily seen is a decided asset. The ability to watch the line as it unrolls toward the target gives the angler a better idea of when to stop its forward flight towards the target.

As soon as the line is stopped and the rod starts to lower, move the line over and put it under the normal stripping finger of the hand gripping the rod handle. If this is accomplished (and it's very easy to do with a little practice), you have complete control of the line from the start of the forward cast until it ends.

Another advantage of using the line hand in this manner to control the shoot is that once the fly arrives at target, you can move it as you wish. Consider a fish lying in a hold along a shoreline. Suddenly something splashes in front of it. The fish looks and just sees a bunch of feathers slowly sinking. But consider the same fish when confronted with a different presentation. If you had stopped the line and had the fly under control just as it struck the surface, you could have had the fly swimming in a realistic manner just as the fish sees it. It is much more likely that this type retrieve will draw a strike.

WATCH THE FLY, NOT THE FISH

How many times have you watched a fly-fishing television show and seen the angler stripping in the fly while the guide is yelling, "He's got it! Strike!"? This happens often when fishing in clear water and there is good visibility. How did the guide know that the fish took the fly when he didn't have the rod in his hands? It's because he was not watching the fish at all. He was doing something more important. He was watching the fly.

If I had to choose one of the most important factors concerning retrieving in clear water, it is that *on the retrieve, you should watch the fly, not the fish.*

THE MAJOR DRY-FLY PRESENTATION FAULTS

There are three prime reasons why many dry-fly fishermen fail, and they are usually not noticed or recognized by the anglers.

Dressing the Fly Improperly — Paste-type dressings are excellent for many types of floating flies. Grasshoppers, spiders, and large flies that need a lot of support to float on the surface of the water can often perform better with an assist from a paste-type dressing. But I feel that putting paste floatant on small dry flies defeats much of the purpose for using them. It's nearly impossible to apply the paste without clumping many of the tiny hackles together.

For that reason, on dry flies size 16 or smaller, I always employ dry-fly oil instead. The oil permits the hackles to remain separated. And you don't normally need to apply a lot of floatant, the oil does such a good job.

But how the dry-fly oil is applied is critical. Remember, it is oil, and when oil is dropped to the water's surface, it creates a prism of color. If you apply dry-fly oil to your fly and immediately make a presentation to the fish, your fly will often be surrounded by a prism resembling a circular rainbow — something a trout has never seen before in its life! Even if you apply the oil and then whip the leader back and forth until the oil is dry, you may still have a small amount of oil that has not properly dried. My suggestion when using dry-fly oil is to make several brisk false casts away from the fish after the oil has been applied. Then drop your fly on the water well away from the fish, drag it underwater, and then false cast hard several more times. This will eliminate the unwanted prism.

False Casting Over the Fish — Another violation of good presentation technique that I see dry-fly fishermen making all the time is false casting over a trout, especially when they are attempting to dry their fly after a drift that has drowned it. Trout have such exceptional eyesight that they can clearly see drifting in the water column (or on top of it) very tiny food organisms that human beings can scarcely perceive. Visualize what happens when an angler picks up his line and fly and makes a series of hard back casts and forward casts to shed water from the drowned fly. That flushed water falls directly below the area where it was whipped from the fly. If the false casts are made over the fish, hundreds of tiny raindrops are thrown from the fly (and the leader) and they fall all around the fish, putting it on the alert. You can see this very plainly if you locate some glare water and false cast a dry fly you have picked off the water over the glare. Scores of tiny dimples appear on the surface as the water droplets fall to the water.

This problem is even more acute when using a braided-butt leader. Such leaders are hollow, and as they float along, the core soaks up water. Then, if the angler picks up the fly and false casts to dry it so that the line and leader travel in the fish's direction, considerably more droplets of water are thrown to the surface near the fish.

When drying your fly (and this is even more important with the braided-butt leaders), lift it carefully from the surface and false cast low and off to the side, allowing any water that is being flushed off the line to fall well away from your quarry.

Lifting Line from the Water Improperly — Lifting the line from the surface is the third major presentation fault of many dry-fly fishermen. It is an especially serious technique flaw whenever fishing calmer water, such as lake surfaces, beaver ponds, spring creeks, or long, still pools.

Surface tension grips any floating fly line as it lays on the water. To visualize how surface tension works, think of your fly line as being lightly glued to thin paper that, in turn, is firmly secured to a surface. If on the back cast you gently raise the rod, the line will silently pull from the light application of glue holding it to the paper. But, if you lift the rod quickly, the paper will tear.

So when you lift your fly line for the back cast, lift it

quickly enough to prevent it from sagging, but not too quickly. *Don't make your back cast until all line is off the water. When the leader butt section begins to leave the surface, you can now make your back cast.*

I estimate that this principle is violated by as many as 80 percent (80 percent!) of dry-fly anglers during a day's fishing. Yet, I think it is one of the most important of all presentation principles.

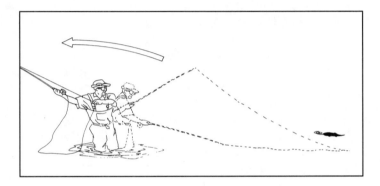

Good Line Pick-Up Technique

Bad Line Pick-Up Technique

BASIC RULES FOR PRESENTATION AND RETRIEVING THE FLY

1. The first cast is the most important one, so make it as perfect as you possibly can.
2. The fly line should never be thrown over or beyond the fish.
3. A correct presentation is one in which the tippet falls in soft waves immediately in back of the fly.
4. When presenting a dry fly, most of the time it should float drag-free from the time the fish first sees it until the take.
5. Major dry-fly presentation faults are 1) dressing the fly improperly; 2) false casting over the fish; and 3) lifting line from the water improperly.
6. When presenting a nymph, try to fish with as short a line as possible.
7. Trout feed much more underwater than on the surface, so getting a drag-free drift with a nymph is essential.
8. There are times when manipulating a dry fly or nymph will help produce a strike.
9. The anatomy and feeding habits of predator fish to a large degree dictate where in the water column the fly should be offered.
10. Generally, the color of the prey species that live on the bottom will closely match the color of the bottom, so when presenting a fly on the bottom, at first offer a pattern that corresponds to bottom coloration.
11. Any fly that is fished underwater should always approach the fish in a natural manner, so that in presenting and retrieving underwater flies, a critical consideration is the angle at which the fly approaches the fish.
12. With underwater flies, there are some situations when a dead drift is better than an activated presentation.

13. When retrieving a streamer or popping bug, the more vulnerable or crippled the offering appears to the fish, the more likely it will strike.
14. With very large fish, a surface bug will often draw a strike when a streamer fly doesn't. The popper creates such a disturbance that it gives the impression of being a larger food source than it actually is.
15. The angle of the fly rod during the retrieve is often critical.
16. Letting go of the line after the shoot is a serious fault, particularly with saltwater presentations.
17. On the retrieve, watch the fly, not the fish.
18. Change your retrieving technique if your present method is not producing results.

OVERLEAF: *John Dusa with steelhead hook-up, Kispiox River, British Columbia.*

CHAPTER FIVE

STRIKING THE FISH

KEEP YOUR ROD TIP LOW

Keeping the rod tip low and pointed at the fish just prior to striking will result in a better hook-up in most situations. Many anglers make the mistake of turning their rod at an angle away from the fish during the retrieve, reducing the amount of distance available to move the rod on the strike. But with the rod pointed directly at the fish, the maximum amount of distance is available to move the rod, and therefore the maximum amount of slack can be removed from the line with rod motion.

DON'T STRIKE TOO HARD

There is a tendency with many anglers to strike too hard, especially if the angler sees or knows he has hooked into a trophy fish. In most situations, unless there is considerable slack in the line, a gentle lifting of the rod while grasping the line firmly with the line hand is all that's needed to set the hook.

I believe that a basic mistake made by many dry-fly fishermen is that they rip the rod backward on the strike too fast and too hard. This results in many tippet breaks.

USE A STRIP STRIKE WITH UNDERWATER FLIES

When fishing underwater flies, almost all but very experienced fly fishermen strike improperly. When they become aware that a fish has taken their underwater fly in shallow water, the normal response of most anglers is to quickly flip the rod tip upward. That's okay if the fish has the fly in its mouth. But if it doesn't, you will lift the fly from the water. If that happens and the fish is fairly close to you, but didn't spook, you may get another chance to throw the fly back into the water. But I wouldn't count on it. Every extra cast thrown near a fish in shallow water lessens your chances of a take.

Anytime that you are retrieving an underwater fly in shallow water and you think that the fish has taken the fly, *never strike upward with the rod tip!* Instead, you can either strike by moving the rod to the side, or use what is called a *strip strike.*

The strip strike is easy. Holding the line in your hand as you are ready to strike, firmly grasp the line with your line hand and simply pull back on it without moving your rod. This technique is most effective if the rod is pointed at the fish and there is no slack in the line. Its advantage, of course, is that if the fish did not have the fly in its mouth (even though you are sure it did) a side or strip strike will only cause the fly to leap just a few inches to one side. Thus the fly remains in front of the fish. And frequently this little hop of the fly on the strip strike will, in and of itself, trigger a second strike.

USE A SLIP STRIKE WITH DRY FLIES

There are writers who have instructed you to gently raise the rod tip when a big trout takes your dry fly. I find that very hard to do. My adrenalin is pumping so fast that I want to rip the lips off the trout, even though I know my fragile tippet is not going to be able to withstand that amount of shock. The gut reaction of most anglers when a trout takes a dry fly is to swiftly raise the rod tip. And that's how we break off tippets.

To prevent break-offs and still allow you to follow your gut reaction of striking as fast as you can, you can resort to a very old technique, which surprisingly is known to very few trout fishermen. It's called a *slip strike*, and with it you'll almost never break even a 7X tippet.

Here's how you make a slip strike. The dry fly comes drifting down toward you and you begin recovering line. Suddenly, the trout rises and takes the fly. Form a large "O" ring by cupping your fingers in a curling motion so that the first two fingers contact the thumb. The line will then be lying loosely inside of the "O" ring formed by your fingers. The instant that your fingers touch the thumb, sweep the rod swiftly to the side or upward. The drag created by the line moving across your fingers and through the rod guides will be more than enough resistance to drive the hook home. But enough slack remains (the line is lying loosely in the line hand) so that it is almost impossible to break the leader. After the line flows through the "O" ring during the sweep of the rod, the line can be immediately trapped after the hook has been set. With a little practice a slip strike can become a very useful tool for trout fishermen.

IN SOME SITUATIONS, STRIKING FORWARD IS BEST

There is a frequent striking problem that occurs when a trout fisherman is casting upstream into a swift current. After the dry fly lands, in order to prevent unwanted slack and get a drag-free drift, the angler will usually raise the rod as the fly drifts toward him. If a strike occurs when the rod is in this elevated position, it's very difficult to set the hook by sweeping backward with the rod.

In these situations, an exactly opposite technique is recommended. Anytime that the rod is near or past vertical during a dry-fly retrieve, and the fish takes, *strike forward* with the rod. The motion is exactly the same as that of making a forward roll cast. The rod sweeps forward and pulls the line and fly toward the angler, setting the hook. Best of all, the instant that the hook is set, the line continues to sweep forward, falling in slack waves. When the trout reacts to the setting of the hook, the slack in the line will prevent it from breaking off the leader. Don't worry about that slack. I've never had a fly fall out after setting the hook in this manner.

ADJUST YOUR STRIKE FOR THE TYPE OF WATER YOU ARE FISHING

Another common mistake made by most trout fishermen when striking with dry flies is that they strike the same way, regardless of the environment that the trout is located in. *You need to adjust the way you strike for the type of water you are fishing.*

If a trout is lying in faster water, such as a riffle, and it sees an insect (or fly) approaching, it sweeps up through the water column, gulps in the fly, and dives to the bottom. It had to move quickly to grab the fly in a quick snatching motion, because it knew that otherwise the fly would disappear in the current. In this situation, set the hook the instant the fish takes the fly.

But examine a trout feeding in a slow-moving pool of water with a calm surface. The trout rises, often drifts back and examines the fly carefully, and then slowly sucks it in. The trout's mouth is open and the fly rides into it on the column of water that is inhaled by the trout. If the angler strikes the moment that the fish takes the fly, while the fly is still in the water column and the trout's mouth is open, the fly can be ripped out of the trout's mouth without ever touching the fish.

In this case, a very slow strike is recommended. In England, where almost all trout waters are slow — especially the chalk streams — for generations local anglers have been saying "God Save The Queen" as the trout takes the fly. They probably don't have the Queen's health on their mind at such moments, but the time it takes them to say those few words gives the fish time enough to suck the fly into its mouth and close it before the strike is made.

STRIKING SLOWLY IS BEST

So if you are going to err in making your strike when fishing dry flies, it's best to err on the slow side. It's surprising how long you can take to set the hook and still connect; and how many fish you'll not hook up if you strike too quickly. Slow striking technique also results in the angler almost always using a more gentle rod motion, thereby reducing the chances of breaking his fragile leader tippet.

WHEN NYMPH FISHING, STRIKE DOWN

When fishing a nymph, the fly is usually cast straight up or at an angle upstream. The angler is attempting to get the nymph to drift downstream in a normal fashion, just as if the current were sweeping it along. He watches either the line, leader or an indicator to see if one of them pauses during the drift. If there is a pause in the drifting line, it perhaps indicates that a trout has the nymph and is examining it. This examination will be quite brief, for the trout will quickly spit out anything it believes to be artificial. During the brief pause, the angler needs to set the hook.

The problem this creates is that many line pauses are actually created not by a fish, but by the nymph contacting a weed, stick, log, bottom or some other underwater obstruction. On such a pause, when the angler sets the hook by sweeping upward with the rod, and it was not a fish after all, the fly has been removed from the water and another cast at close quarters has to be made. Of course this is undesirable.

But what if you could strike at every pause, and set the hook well if it were a trout, but not remove the fly from the water if it were not? That would be an ideal nymphing situation. And it is possible.

Make your cast and watch the fly as it drifts down to you. If there is a pause, snap sharply *downward* with the rod. *This will cause the rod tip to first whip upward and then downward.* I know this sounds crazy, but assemble a fly rod and hold it out in front of you. Now snap downward and watch the tip. First it goes up, and then down.

What this action accomplishes is to allow the nymph fisherman to strike on many pauses that are not fish, and since the downward strike only zips the fly a few inches through the water, if there's no take the fly is not out of the water and out of action, but is continuing to drift through the pool.

ON LARGE AND TOUGH-MOUTHED FISH, STRIKE WITH THE ROD BUTT

Striking many large, powerful fish, or those with a tough mouth, calls for employing a different striking method. When we strike most freshwater fish, we actually strike with the rod tip. That is, we raise the rod tip to set the hook. This is usually accomplished by either lifting the forearm or snapping the wrist to set the hook.

That won't work with most very powerful fish or those with extra-hard or tough mouths. For example, a tarpon has a mouth inside like a metal bucket and it takes considerable force to drive a sharp hook into that bony interior. Similarly, billfish and many other tough-mouthed fish require a different technique for striking.

When striking many large and powerful fish, and all tough-mouthed fish, you need to drive the hook home by striking with the BUTT of the rod.

Let's take an example of a tarpon that has just inhaled the fly. A wrist strike would be futile, because as the heavy tarpon rod is snapped up and jars against the fish, there's a good chance that your wrist, which does not have a particularly powerful muscle structure, will more than likely collapse. Instead, put both your arms close to the body, and turn to one side or the other, keeping the rod tip pointed almost at the tarpon. This assures that you are using your very powerful back and leg muscles and the very strong butt section of your rod to help drive the hook deeply into the fish's mouth.

BASIC RULES FOR STRIKING THE FISH
1. Whenever possible, keep the rod pointed low and at the fish just prior to setting the hook.
2. Don't strike too hard.
3. With underwater flies in shallow water, never strike upward with the rod.
4. When dry-fly fishing, a slip strike is often best.
5. If the fly is drifting rapidly toward the angler, slack is accumulating and the rod is usually elevated to get rid of that slack. If a fish takes with the rod in this position, roll cast forward with the rod tip.
6. When a trout takes a dry fly, the speed of the current affects how you strike.
7. When nymph fishing, many times driving the rod tip down towards the water is best.
8. When striking most large or powerful fish, and all tough-mouthed fish, never strike with the rod tip. Instead, strike with the butt of the rod.

OVERLEAF: *Val Atkinson with a large brown trout captured and released on the South Island of New Zealand.*

CHAPTER SIX

FIGHTING THE FISH

The most important factor in fighting any big fish on a light rod is never to allow a jerk to occur on the fragile leader. Steady pressure rarely is responsible for breaking off a fish. It's the sudden jerk that does — and I often claim it's the jerk on the wrong end! Take a piece of 3X tippet material and try to slowly pull it apart and break it. Under this steady pressure you'll be amazed at how strong the tippet is. Now, repeat the operation, but instead of a steady pull, give a sharp jerk, and the tippet will part instantly. This is a fact you must be constantly in tune with when fighting a large fish on a fragile tippet.

USE OF THE REEL'S DRAG MECHANISM

A major factor in fighting fish is proper use of a drag, an adjustable restraining device that prevents the escaping fish from breaking the line. Most saltwater fly reels, as well as the freshwater reels that are used for fighting larger fish, such as salmon, are equipped with a drag device. There are different schools of thought on just how the adjustable tension or restraint on a drag should be set.

How smoothly a drag releases line is important and all good drags will do this. For that release, a drag is said to have a *starting* and a *running* drag. Starting drag simply means the drag won't release line until enough pressure is applied. Running drag is the amount of resistance needed to keep the spool in motion against the drag. In almost all reels, it will take more pressure on the line to get a drag started than it does to keep it running, just as it's much harder to get a stalled car moving than it is to keep it moving. Drags on fly reels work the same way.

Some reels have a much lower starting drag than others, and they are recommended. If you are considering buying a new reel and are comparing several models, attach a scale to a fly line attached to each of the reels being considered and check them to see which has a lower starting drag.

Fly reels with drags come in two designs: direct drive and anti-reverse. Direct drive means that when the fish runs the reel handle will turn, freeing line. Anti-reverse reels, on the other hand, allow the angler to hold onto the reel handle while the fish is pulling off line. With either design, how hard the fish has to pull to get line is controlled by the amount of drag tension that the angler sets on the reel's drag mechanism.

There are some fishing situations in which an anti-reverse reel is not recommended. In bonefishing, for example, the light tippets that are used require that you set the drag tension for no more than a pound on a straight pull. But if a bonefish runs off a lot of line, the light drag tension you have set on the slip clutch of the anti-reverse reel may not be enough to retrieve the line and the fish. The drag will simply slip. In such situations a direct drive reel is much better.

If anglers make a mistake in setting drags, it's that they establish too much drag, which increases the starting drag factor and helps break lines. You can check the amount of drag pressure you have established on your reel by attaching a scale to the line end and then pulling on the scale until the drag releases. Note on the scale what the starting drag is and what the running drag is. A very good guide for most species is never to set the starting drag for more than 20 percent of the test of the line, and a 15 percent ratio is even better.

You may encounter a few situations in which a heavy drag setting may be necessary. In saltwater, for example, if you are fishing over a wreck or a coral reef, around bridge pilings, night fishing bridges, or anywhere that you must not allow the fish to get into the structure, then a heavier drag setting is advised.

But whenever the fish can be fought in relatively open water, if you er · on a drag setting, err on the light side.

For bonefisl my personal way of setting the starting drag tension is ₁o grip the fly line directly in front of the reel as firmly as I can between my lips. Then I adjust the drag until I can just pull off line. This is usually less than a pound of direct pull.

For sailfish, a drag setting of more than one pound of pull is necessary if you are using leader tippets testing at 16 pounds or less. This is because a sailfish runs off such a terrific amount of line at very high speed, creating such great water tension against the line, that if there is less than one pound of drag setting, the leader will break.

It's important to understand that there are times when you need to reduce or back off the drag, too. If you have a full spool of line adjusted to a drag of say, one pound, and then the spool is more than half emptied by the run of a fish, the amount of drag now required to pull line from the reel could easily be three times that much, or three pounds. Therefore, if you encounter a very long run from a fish, it's wise to reduce the drag tension a bit.

When a large fish is finally brought to boatside, there is little margin of error should the fish suddenly bolt away. So when the fish is close to the boat and preparations are being made to land it, it's a good idea to back off slightly on the drag. That way, should the fish suddenly try to escape, the rod can be pointed at the fish and there will be no sudden jolt on the line as the starting and then running drags begin to function.

One other factor needs to be considered when using the drag to fight the fish — the angle of the rod during the battle. When a rod is bowed under pressure from the fish, the line is not flowing against the rod, but from one guide to another guide. The more deeply the rod is bowed during the fight, the more the line binds against each of the guides. This creates considerable drag pressure.

You can conduct an experiment to check this out. String a fly line through the rod guides and attach it to a spring scale. Using the spring scale, adjust the drag tension on your reel until you have a starting drag of one pound. Now have a companion slowly elevate the rod under tension. As

Adjust Drag Pressure After Fishing

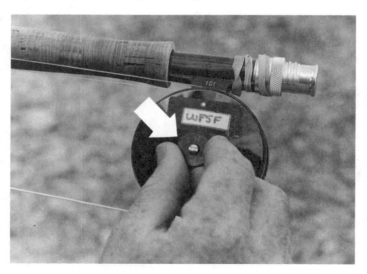

the rod starts bowing, the scale will show that an increase of poundage results before the drag begins to slip. The binding of the fly line against the guides actually results in more drag tension than a straight pull off the reel.

That is why it's important when a fish surges away from the angler that the rod tip be dropped in the direction of the fish. This allows the line to flow straight off the reel, not binding on the guides, and the lowest amount of drag pressure will be required to get the drag slipping.

Finally, an important point about setting drags. Almost all drags (spinning, fly, or conventional reels) are comprised of alternating soft and hard washers. Your drag will only function smoothly as long as the softer drag washers remain soft. If you screw down the adjustment nut on any kind of reel and allow it to remain that way for long periods of time, that tension slowly crushes the softness from the washers and a jerky drag will result. *So make it a habit always to back off the drag tension on any reel at the end of the day's fishing.*

LINE CONTROL DURING THE FIGHT

It is immediately after the strike that the fish will usually exhibit its wildest behavior in attempting to escape. This is one of the two times when fish are most frequently lost. The other is at the very end of the battle.

So be prepared to instantly feed line as soon as you stick the hook in the fish. For fast-running fish there is a definite technique that will help you in this regard.

When a fast-running fish takes off after the strike, frequently the line lying at the angler's feet gets tangled, or it wraps around the butt of the rod as most of the line slips through the guides. To prevent these problems, try this. The moment you have firmly set the hook *forget the fish and concentrate on clearing loose line.*

To do this, as soon as you hook up, form an "O" ring with the fingers of the line hand, touching the first two fingers against the thumb, and use this as a giant rod guide to feed the line down at your feet so that it comes up through the guides. Often you'll see a tangle coming and you can either shake the line to clear it, or handle it in some other manner so that it finally clears through the guides.

At the same time that you form the "O" ring with the line hand, cock your rod hand inward so that *the butt of the rod is pressed firmly against your forearm just back of the wrist. Then turn the rod hand downward and outward.* This places the butt of the rod firmly against the forearm and by rotating the hand outward, you place the reel on the outside of your forearm, which will prevent the line traveling up from your feet from tangling in the reel or slipping under the end of the rod butt.

How you clear the last few feet of line being pulled by the escaping fish is also important. Make your line hand move toward the butt or stripping guide as the last part of the line is being cleared. This insures that the final portion of line flows cleanly through the guides.

A very special problem sometimes arises when an escaping fish is pulling line rapidly from beneath you: a tangle occurs in the line lying at your feet. To avoid this problem, experienced anglers use extra-large snake and ring guides on their rods to avoid fouling. But occasionally a larger loop or tangle sweeps toward the guides. Usually such a large tangle will go through the first two guides. But when the rod is bent in a deep curve, the fly line doesn't follow the rod blank, but is stretched taut from guide to guide. In this situation, the tangle will usually jam against a wire snake guide, and the tippet breaks.

Many times you can prevent such a break-off by *turning the rod upside-down.* What happens then is that instead of

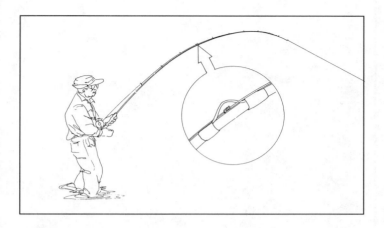

Turn Rod Upside-Down

jumping from guide to guide, the line and knot run along the smooth rod blank and enter the snake guides at their base, the largest part of a snake guide's opening. It doesn't work all the time, but it has frequently saved a fish for me.

PUMPING AND WINDING TECHNIQUES

If you are a trout or bass fisherman, you know that you can land just about any fish you'll ever hook simply by winding line in with the reel handle. But this is not possible with the more powerful fish species, such as Atlantic salmon, steelhead, large northern pike, or almost all the larger saltwater species. When fighting such fish, you must recover line by pumping and winding.

Proper pumping is not usually practiced by most fishermen. They make long upward or backward sweeps of the rod, then drop the rod toward the fish and wind in accumulated slack. This is not good technique.

OVERLEAF: *Matching the hatch on Silver Creek, Idaho.*

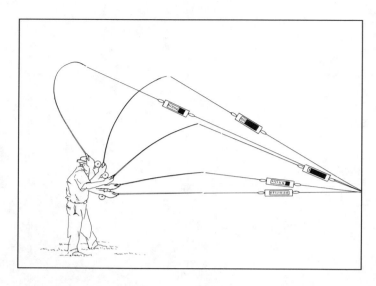

Rod Pressure on Fish Decreases Above 45 Degrees

You can learn a lot about proper pumping technique by attaching the leader to a spring scale. Then have someone trap the line against the rod butt and begin to raise the rod. As the rod starts its upward motion, the drag will increase. But once the lower portion of the rod gets a little beyond 45 degrees, the amount of pressure being applied starts dropping back. As the lower rod butt reaches an angle of 90 degrees or more, the amount of pressure that is being applied really starts falling away.

This demonstrates that making a long up and down motion of the rod is actually serving to reduce the pressure you are applying on the fish. Instead, make a series of short pumps, recovering only a tiny bit of line each time you lower the rod tip.

When pumping, it's also important not to drop the rod tip too fast. If you do, slack occurs that could cause prob-

Pump and Wind Technique

lems. Instead, *always keep a little bend in the rod tip as you lower the rod and reel in line*. Every time the fish bolts, by following this technique of dropping the rod and pointing the rod tip at the fish to reduce starting drag, you can subdue some really huge fish.

ROD TECHNIQUE DURING THE FIGHT

Rod angle is also very important during the fight. If the hooked fish is in the current below and you hold your rod straight up, you are actually allowing the fish to rest. Try this. Hook a stick on your fly and let it float downstream from you. Then elevate the rod to a vertical position. Note how much pressure the current against the stick puts on your rod, yet the stick does nothing.

Most of the time during the fight with a fish either the fish or you should be getting line. But there are a few occasions when neither one of you is able to do anything but hold on. Sometimes the only way you can land a strong fish on a fragile leader is to simply let the fish burn up enough energy until the time when you can apply enough pressure to control it and bring it to your feet.

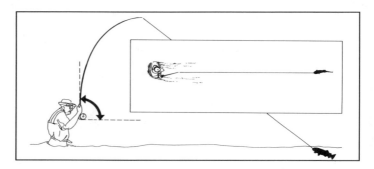

Rod Technique: During Fight

Anytime that a fish is under 35 to 40 feet away, you should swing your rod to apply side pressure opposite the direction the fish is swimming. For example, a fish is slowly moving to your left. Drop the rod to your right and parallel

Rod Technique: Side Pressure to Right

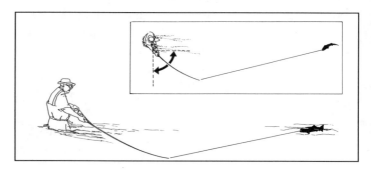

to the water. This move pulls the fish off balance and to one side. The fish will struggle against this pressure, but you should be able to turn it slowly so that it will begin swimming to the right in the direction of the pressure you are exerting on the line.

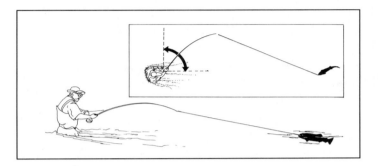

Rod Technique: Side Pressure to Left

As soon as it is apparent that the fish is swimming to the right, swing the rod over and low to the left. This repeats the operation. By constantly turning the fish one way and the other — with the fish all the while fighting that resistance — you can wear a fish down faster than by any other fighting technique I know of.

In fact, by using this side-pressure technique on strong fish like steelhead, Atlantic and Pacific salmon, or fish caught in the surf, you can often zigzag the fish's swimming course so that it actually swims up onto the beach.

Incidentally, if you have finally gotten a large saltwater fish right to your boot tops in the surf, watch the waves. Usually about every seventh wave is a little larger than the others. When you see a larger wave coming, get ready, and then move swiftly up on the beach, placing pressure on the fish. Your rod pressure and the large wave will frequently combine to carry the fish up on the beach, stranding it as the waves recede.

BOWING AND DIPPING TECHNIQUES

A fish underwater cannot move as swiftly as it can when airborne, because of the resistance of the water against its body. But when a fish rises above the surface (whether it is a tarpon, rainbow trout, or bass) it can snap its body violently back and forth and exert such pressure that the hook may be pulled free or the tippet breaks. To prevent this from happening, you need to feed *controlled* slack while the fish is in the air.

There are two methods for doing this. One is the traditional way, bowing to the fish. The other is by dipping the rod. Either one works, although I prefer dipping, since you get better slack line control with it. Here's how to work these techniques.

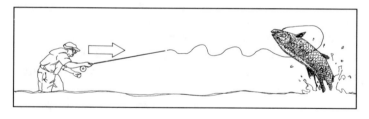

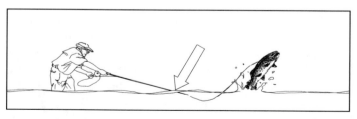

Bowing (top) and Dipping Rod (bottom) to Leaping Fish

The fish leaps out of the water. The angler sees this and if he employs the bowing technique, as he bows he points and pushes the rod in the direction of the fish. But sometimes in bowing, the slack line wavering in the air as the fish rocks back and forth will tangle in the head of the fish, or around the rod tip. With the dipping technique, the angler points the rod at the fish *but he places the tip of the rod a few inches under the surface of the water.* Thus in dipping, most of the line remains under the water in a gentle bend, and while there is still some slack remaining, it is under better control. Whichever method you prefer, bowing or dipping, when the fish returns to the water, you should again apply conventional rod pressure.

BASIC RULES FOR FIGHTING THE FISH

1. Before you make your presentation consider how you will fight and land the fish.
2. When fighting strong fish on fragile leaders, never allow a jerk to occur on the line or leader.
3. The fish's most frantic moments usually occur immediately after the strike. Be aware that the fish may bolt away. So be prepared!
4. When fighting larger fish, you can't just reel them in. Use a rod pumping motion to draw them closer.
5. Rod angle is very important when fighting a fish and must be changed to meet different conditions during the battle.
6. When fish jump, throw slack while the fish is in the air, either by bowing to the fish or dipping the rod.

OVERLEAF: *Bob Lewis fly fishing for trout in the fall on the Madison River, Yellowstone National Park, Wyoming.*

CHAPTER SEVEN

LANDING AND RELEASING THE FISH

If you are really a sportsman, you will try to land and release your fish as quickly as possible. This means using the strongest leader that gives both you and the fish a chance. I've seen fly fishermen, using 8X tippets on a 12-inch trout, fight the poor fish for 10 or 15 minutes because the angler was afraid to put any pressure on the fragile leader. When the fish was finally landed, it was in such poor condition that I doubt whether it survived.

GET THE FISH'S HEAD OUT OF WATER

When a fish has been fought hard and brought to within a rod length, make an attempt to get its head out of the water, if possible. This helps to immobilize the fish so that it can be landed more easily. This is best accomplished by lowering the rod tip, reeling in slack, and then physically lifting the fish's head a few inches above the surface.

IF POSSIBLE, DON'T TOUCH THE FISH

If it's possible, don't touch the fish if you are going to release it. There are several methods available to get the hook out of the fish without handling it. One method, that is very effective when fishing for trout with barbless hooks and small nymphs or dry flies, was shown to me by John

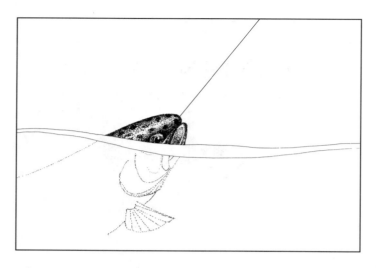

Lift Fish's Head from Water

Goddard, one of England's leading anglers and angling writers, and one of the two best trout fly fishermen I have ever known. In his country, where the banks are high along many of the chalk streams, getting down to the fish for the release is sometimes pretty difficult.

John accomplishes his release this way. If the hook is inside the mouth of the fish (it doesn't work well if the hook is outside the mouth), John strips in the line and leader *until the rod tip meets snugly against the bend in the hook.* This means the tip may even be just inside the trout's mouth. Grasping the leader and holding it taut, so that the hook bend is held firmly against the tip of the rod, John makes a quick little shove with the rod toward the trout. If the hook is held taut by the rod tip, the barbless hook is backed out of the flesh and the trout swims away.

Another method of handling many freshwater fish as well as small saltwater species, such as bonefish, is to bring

Releasing Fish with Hemostats

the fish close enough so that you can slide your hand down the leader and grasp the tippet a few inches above the hook. This helps you control the fish's movement. Then, using either hemostats or needle-nose pliers, grasp the hook *by the bend*, and turn the tool so that the point of the hook is directed toward the bottom. This will lift the fish slightly, and it will slide off the hook. If there is a barb, you may need to "bounce" the fish gently before it falls free. With this method you can quickly release a fish.

NETTING AND GAFFING FISH

I don't like to net fish because nets can damage the fish's eyes and cause protective slime to be removed from its flesh. I also don't like to gaff a fish, but if there is a need to net or gaff a fish, you should follow a couple of simple rules.

First, if your reel has a drag, it should be backed off a little just before you capture the fish, because there is little margin for error if a fish surges against a short line when it is at your feet.

And, most importantly, you should stand behind the netter or gaffer to give him a better shot at the fish; but at the same time you need to maintain such a position that the fish is clearly visible to you at all times. Then if the fish attempts to escape, you can drop the rod tip toward the fish and take necessary action.

LEAVE FISH IN THE WATER AS MUCH AS POSSIBLE

Fish can't breathe air, so if you intend to revive the fish, keep it in the water as much as possible. If you are going to take photos, then get all your camera equipment ready before lifting the fish from the water. Shoot quickly and return the fish to the water as soon as possible.

TECHNIQUES FOR LIFTING FISH

There is a simple way to lift almost all fish from the water without using a net. Aussie guides showed it to me when we were shooting a fly-fishing film in Australia and New Guinea a few years ago. They call it the comfort lift. In more than a month of fishing, no nets or gaffs were ever used, and we caught some *BIG* fish. Here's how it works.

Bring the fish close. Slide your hand under the body *from the belly side* to prevent being stuck by the fish's spines. *The key is to locate the center of the fish's weight (not its length).* Once you've located this spot, cup your hand under the fish and lift it gently from the water. The fish will lie in your hand as if drugged. You can then remove the hook, carry the fish to another place, and release it. It's astonishing how easily this works.

Another method is to grasp the fish gently and turn it upside-down. Again, if you haven't tried this, you'll be amazed. The fish lies there motionless and you can remove the hook and release the fish. Biologists I have talked to about the comfort and upside-down lifts don't believe these lifts harm the fish at all.

TECHNIQUES FOR REVIVING FISH

I have revived many fish that others thought were going to die. What revives a fish, unless it is really in bad shape, is to get oxygen flowing across its gills. Many people will hold a fish with the head pointing into the current and gently rock the fish back and forth. But with this procedure, the only water flowing across the fish's gills is the little that enters the mouth.

Instead — if the fish doesn't have a mouth full of sharp teeth — try this method. Grasp the lower lip of the fish with the thumb and finger. Hold the tail firmly with the other hand. Then make sharp *backward* sweeps so that the fish is jolted backwards in the water. This causes its gills to flare open widely and water pours across them. It's amazing how much better you can revive a fish with this technique.

Reviving Fish

TECHNIQUES FOR RELEASING FISH

Never release a fish until you feel it can swim well enough on its own. If in doubt, let it try to swim away. If it's having trouble, grab it and spend more time reviving it. Also, *never, never, throw a fish back*. This stuns the fish and often makes it prey to a nearby predator. Always put the fish back into the water gently.

If possible, you never want to release a fish where you can't recapture it. If a fish has to be released in deeper water, get it in as good a shape as possible and then let it go. But have an oar, paddle, boat pole, fishing rod or some other long object at hand. If the fish turns belly-up or has trouble swimming, touch it with the long object. Frequently that is enough stimulus to get the fish going again.

BASIC RULES FOR LANDING AND RELEASING THE FISH

1. Sportsmen should try to land their fish quickly.
2. Get the fish's head out of water at fight's end.
3. When removing the hook, don't touch fish if possible.
4. If the fish is to be gaffed or netted, back off on the drag and stand behind the netter or gaffer, but in a position so that you can clearly see the fish.
5. Keep fish in the water as much as possible.
6. Use the comfort or upside-down lifts when handling fish out of water.
7. To revive a fish that doesn't have sharp teeth, hold it underwater, grip the lower jaw in one hand and the tail in the other, and rock the fish back and forth.
8. Don't release a fish until it is in good condition.
9. Never release a fish where you can't recover it.
10. If you have to release a fish in deeper water and it appears to be in trouble, touch it firmly with some object at hand to startle and revive it.

INDEX